W9-ACD-306

The ART OF THE
PERFECT SAUCE

The ART OF THE PERFECT SAUCE

75 RECIPES TO TAKE YOUR DISHES FROM ORDINARY TO EXTRAORDINARY

LORILYNN BAUER & RAMIN GANESHRAM

PAGE STREET
PUBLISHING CO.

PAGE STREET
PUBLISHING CO.

First published in 2018 by
Page Street Publishing Co.
27 Congress Street, Suite 105
Salem, MA 01970
www.pagestreetpublishing.com

Distributed by Macmillan, sales in Canada by The Canadian Manda Group.

22 21 20 19 18   1 2 3 4 5

ISBN-13: 978-1-62414-504-9

ISBN-10: 1-62414-504-3

Library of Congress Control Number: 2017943500

Cover and book design by Page Street Publishing Co.

Photography by Allison Lehman

Printed and bound in China

As a member of 1% for the Planet, Page Street Publishing protects our planet by donating to nonprofits like The Trustees, which focuses on local land conservation. Learn more at onepercentfortheplanet.org.

TO BRITTANY, ADDISON, SOPHIA,
BLYTHE AND MADELINE WHO INSPIRE US TO
MAKE EVERY MEAL A DELICIOUS ADVENTURE.

Contents

SAUCES FOR VEGETABLES AND PASTA 119

SAUCES FOR DESSERT 145

DIPPING SAUCES 173

INTRODUCTION

One of the first things you learn in culinary school after how to make a proper stock is how to make sauces. This was true for us both, even though we went to different schools—Lorilynn to Culinary Institute of America and Ramin to Institute of Culinary Education. We have pursued different culinary paths as cooks—Lorilynn as a restaurant and private chef with a six-season stint on Iron Chef America as Cat Cora's sous-chef, and Ramin as a food journalist and cookbook writer.

Despite this, we've always managed to come together to make some epic meals. In those marathon cooking sessions, time and again we always went back to the importance of a great sauce. Considered a foundation of fine cuisine, sauces can elevate even the most well prepared dish to new heights. In fact, in traditional French kitchens, the position of saucier or sauce-making chef was a profession unto itself and one of honor and distinction.

For many of us, the sauces we learned in culinary school seemed already past their prime by the time we came along. These were the five traditional Mother Sauces of French cuisine: Béchamel, a milk sauce thickened with white roux; Sauce Tomat, or tomato sauce; Veloute, a white stock thickened with white roux; Sauce Esapagnole or Brown Sauce—what most people would call gravy; and Hollandaise Sauce, an emulsion of clarified butter and egg yolks.

Heavy, creamy and thick, these sauces seem, at first blush, to have no place in modern cooking with its emphasis on fresh, whole ingredients prepared with a light hand to allow their inherent flavors to shine through.

The fact is, though, nothing could be further from the truth. Even if rarely used on their own—particularly in a home kitchen—when amended or adapted, the French Mother Sauces are the basis for other sauces we all know and love. Mayonnaise and its garlicky counterpart aioli is an emulsification based upon the same principles as a good Hollandaise. If you love true Mac 'n' cheese, thank Sauce Mornay—essentially Béchamel fortified with cheese. Many savory glazes are built out of Sauce Espagnole.

More than the sauces themselves, it is their technique that has the most value—and allows us to experiment with a wide variety of ingredients to design the fresh new sauces that you will find in this book.

You'll find that, for the most part, the sauces we've created here are extremely simple to make and span a variety of techniques that, once mastered, will empower you to invent unique sauces of your own. A handy Sauce Table (page 18) indicates where sauces can serve double or even triple duty across a variety of proteins and vegetables. An additional section for dessert sauces is sure to appeal to your sweet tooth as well.

One final note: Each recipe contains prep times and cooking times. Of course, these may vary slightly based on your own skill level and kitchen equipment—modern appliances can have quite a range of power. As such, we suggest using the visual and doneness cues as your primary guideline for the completed sauce.

—LORILYNN & RAMIN

Mastering Sauces

A TECHNIQUE PRIMER

THE FIRST STEP: A WELL-MADE STOCK

One of the first and foundational techniques learned by culinary students is how to make a rich and flavorful stock using meat bones and trimmings. Stocks are an important building block for sauces, and you'll find that many, although not all, of the sauces in this book make use of vegetable, chicken or meat stock.

While stocks are easily purchased at any grocery store, the ones you make yourself are going to be fresher and feature the flavor profiles you most favor. The recipes we provide are basic stock recipes, but you may certainly increase any of the aromatic ingredients (onions, garlic, carrot, celery or spices) to suit your taste. You will notice, though, that we never put salt in stocks and for a good reason: As stocks are boiled down in sauces, any salt they contain will intensify and potentially adversely change the sauce flavor.

Stock is also excellent as a soup starter or to replace water in stews or as a braising liquid for meats. Because stock can be made ahead and refrigerated for up to 5 days and frozen for 2 weeks, we encourage you to have a go at making your own—you'll taste the difference in your sauces.

VEGETABLE STOCK

Vegetable stock is suitable both for vegetarian and meat-based sauces. Keep in mind that it is a darker stock than chicken stock and this will affect the color of your final preparation.

MAKES: about 2 quarts (2 L)   **PREP TIME:** 10 minutes   **COOKING TIME:** 1 hour 50 minutes

5 lbs (2.2 kg) chopped mixed carrots, zucchini or yellow squash, green beans and red bell pepper

1 large onion, chopped

1 tbsp (15 ml) olive oil

7 garlic gloves, peeled and smashed

1 bay leaf

1 tsp (4 g) whole black peppercorns

½ bunch fresh parsley

5 sprigs fresh thyme

2½ quarts (10 cups [2.5 L]) cold water

Preheat the oven to 450°F (232°C). Toss the vegetables and onion in olive oil in an ovenproof dish or baking sheet. Roast the vegetables for 15 minutes, stirring once, then stir in the garlic and roast for 5 minutes more.

Place the vegetables and the bay leaf, peppercorns, parsley and thyme in a large stockpot with the water. Simmer on low for 1½ hours.

Ladle the stock through a fine mesh sieve into heat-safe/freezer-safe containers. Refrigerate for up to 1 week or freeze immediately for up to 3 weeks.

CHICKEN STOCK

Chicken stock is truly the multipurpose stock of them all. It can be used for all manner of sauces from vegetable to poultry to meat or fish.

MAKES: about 4 quarts (4 L)   **PREP TIME:** 15 minutes   **COOKING TIME:** 3 hours 25 minutes

8 lbs (3.6 kg) chicken carcasses or bones

2 large onions, chopped

4 large carrots, chopped

4 ribs celery, chopped

1 head of garlic, peeled and crushed

4 bay leaves

1 tbsp (13 g) whole black peppercorns

½ bunch fresh parsley

8 sprigs thyme

8 quarts (32 cups [7.5 L]) cold water

Preheat the oven to 450°F (232°C). Place the chicken bones or carcasses in an oven-safe dish and add the onions, carrots, celery and garlic and roast for 25 minutes.

Put the roasted bones, vegetables, bay leaves, peppercorns, parsley, thyme and water in a 12-quart (12-L) stockpot. Place the pot a little off center on the burner. Simmer on low for 3 hours, skimming impurities that collect on the side of the pot.

Ladle the stock through a fine mesh sieve into heat-safe/freezer-safe containers. Refrigerate for up to 5 days or freeze immediately for up to 2 weeks. Skim any solidified fat from the chilled stock before using.

MEAT STOCK

Meat stocks—often now popularly called bone broth—are richly flavored and add intensity to sauces. They can be overpowering for poultry or fish sauces, so we most often call for their use with meat dishes.

MAKES: about 4 quarts (4 L)   **PREP TIME:** 15 minutes   **COOKING TIME:** 3 hours 25 minutes

8 lbs (3.6 kg) meaty bones from beef, veal, lamb or venison

1 tbsp (15 ml) tomato paste

2 large onions, chopped

4 large carrots, chopped

4 ribs celery, chopped

1 head of garlic, peeled and crushed

4 bay leaves

1 tbsp (13 g) whole black peppercorns

½ bunch fresh parsley

8 sprigs thyme

8 quarts (32 cups [7.5 L]) cold water

Preheat the oven to 450°F (232°C). Place the bones in an oven safe baking dish and roast for 15 minutes. Stir in the tomato paste, mixing well so that all the bones are coated.

Add the onions, carrots, celery and garlic and roast for 10 minutes more.

Put the bones, vegetables, bay leaves, peppercorns, parsley, thyme and water in a 12-quart (12-L) stockpot. Place the pot a little off center of the burner. Simmer on low for 3 hours, skimming impurities that collect on the side of the pot.

Ladle the stock through a fine mesh sieve into heat-safe/freezer-safe containers. Refrigerate for up to 5 days or freeze immediately for up to 2 weeks. Skim any fat that rises to the surface of the chilled stock before using.

A SAUCE PRIMER

THE TECHNIQUES

Pan Sauce

Pan sauces are quick and easy sauces that, once mastered, can elevate even the simplest preparation. They are very much sauces "of the moment" because they usually make use of the drippings or *fond* that comes from searing a protein in a hot pan as the basis for the sauce's flavor. The process for a pan sauce is always the same even if the individual ingredients differ.

1. Sauté aromatics such as onion, garlic, shallot, chives or leaks in the grease remaining in or added to your frying pan.

2. Deglaze the pan using an acidic liquid. Wine is usually used, but vinegar and citrus juices may be used as well.

3. Add stock to the pan along with any additional flavoring agents such as herbs, dried fruits or spices other than salt. Reduce the mixture until there are bubbles across the surface of the pan and the sauce reaches the nappé stage (see photo page 16).

4. Add butter to the pan and swirl to melt. This gives the sauce a sheen and velvety texture. If you are straining your sauce, add the butter afterward.

Simmer Sauces

Simmer sauces are those in which foods can be actually cooked or finished for flavor. Simmer sauces are made by combining ingredients that are allowed to simmer so that their flavors meld. They can be made ahead of time and stored, refrigerated, until they are used. Some examples of simmer sauces are Everyone's Favorite Tikka Masala (page 57) or Fesanjan (Persian Pomegranate and Walnut Sauce page 54).

Thickened Sauces

Thickened sauces are sauces that are usually made from available drippings that are then thickened with an agent such as flour, cornstarch or, sometimes, arrowroot. Thanksgiving gravy made from turkey drippings is a thickened sauce with which everyone is familiar and our Never Fail Go-To Gravy (page 53) is a good example.

Emulsified Sauces

Emulsified sauces work by forcing oil and water together so that they blend without separating. This process if often aided by the use of an acid such as vinegar or lemon juice. Emulsified sauces can be cooked or cold (raw). Examples of cooked sauces are classic Hollandaise Sauce and Roasted Garlic Beurre Blanc (page 76). Cold sauces include common mayonnaise and Spicy Red Pepper Aioli (page 133).

Whisked Sauces

Whisked sauces use friction to temporarily bring ingredients together, most often to suspend an oil in liquid. Vinaigrettes like Saffron Mace Vinaigrette (page 84) are a good example of a whisked sauce.

(continued)

Gastriques/Agrodolces

Both gastriques and agrodolces are sweet and sour sauces that combine sugar, honey or other sweetening agent with an acidic liquid, most commonly vinegar, and flavorings that are simmered together into a syrup. Agrodolce, which translates to sour-sweet, is traditional to Italian cuisine. Gastriques are French and originally were used as a flavoring for other sauces and often comprised a bit of stock. Today the two terms are usually interchangeable.

Mignonettes

Mignonettes are sauces created specifically for raw oysters though they can be used for other raw shellfish such as clams as well. Mignonettes always make use of cracked black pepper and shallots, but the type of vinegar can change. Sichuan Peppercorn Mignonette (page 63) is a good variation on the theme.

Compound Butter

With it wide variety of uses, compound butter is a handy sauce to have around. Simply a mixture of softened unsalted butter, spices or other seasonings that are then re-chilled to firmness, a pat of these flavored butters have been classically used on steaks and chops and steamed vegetables or as the foundation for a butter-based sauce. Sweetened compound butters are excellent on toast, muffins, waffles and pancakes as well or used as a foundation in dessert sauces. Five-Spice Brown Sugar Compound Butter (page 171) is a good example of a compound butter that can do double duty for sweet and savory uses.

THE THICKENERS

Roux

Roux is a thickening agent that is made from cooking fat and flour together. The fat can be oil, melted grease or butter. The flour is added and the two are cooked together to the desired degree of doneness. There are light roux, which are only cooked enough to take the raw taste out of the flour all the way to extremely dark roux. The darker the roux, the more nutty or even bitter the taste the roux will lend to the dish it's thickening. Roux are usually made as the starting point of a thickened dish, with liquid such as stock or milk (as in Béchamel Sauce) added to the roux once it is made.

Beurre Manie

Beurre Manie is equal parts flour and butter kneaded together in a process that coats all the butter particles in flour. It is an excellent quick method for thickening a sauce, stew or soup. Beurre Manie can be made and kept, refrigerated, in an airtight container for several weeks so that it is easily at hand for a quick thickening agent. It is particularly good for thickening gravies without forming lumps.

Cornstarch

Cornstarch can be an effective thickening agent for sauces, especially those that are more translucent in color as it does not make a sauce opaque as flour does. Cornstarch is also good for both savory and sweet sauces. It is used by dissolving cornstarch in an equal amount of water to create a liquid that is roughly the consistency of heavy cream. This slurry is then added to boiling liquid and then the heat is reduced to a simmer to be stirred while it thickens.

Flour

Plain flour can be used as a thickening agent although it is generally not as effective as cornstarch and can be lumpy. We find that adding a very small amount of flour to a sauce, using a handled, fine mesh sieve while whisking the sauce vigorously is the most effective way to make use of flour as a thickening agent.

Arrowroot

Arrowroot is a powder made from various tropical roots and tubers that have thickening properties. It is used as a flour in gluten-free baked goods and is an excellent non-animal gelatin. Arrowroot provides a thickening quality that is even more translucent than cornstarch but is used in the same manner: by whisking together equal amounts of arrowroot and liquid and then adding to the desired preparation.

THE SAUCE TABLE

The following chart is a handy guide to see which sauce can do double or even triple duty across proteins and vegetables. We encourage you to experiment as well.

THE SAUCES	POULTRY	MEAT	FISH	VEGETABLES AND PASTA	DESSERTS	DIPPING
Coconut Cream and Turmeric Sauce (page 29)	✔		✔			
Savory Yuzu and Ginger Sauce (page 30)	✔		✔			✔
Hoisin Habañero Sauce (page 33)	✔	✔		✔		✔

THE SAUCES	POULTRY	MEAT	FISH	VEGETABLES AND PASTA	DESSERTS	DIPPING
Smoked Tomato and Marcona Almond Romesco (page 34)	✔		✔			
Savory Cashew and Cardamom Cream Sauce (Korma) (page 37)	✔		✔	✔		
Hot Honey Sauce (page 38)	✔		✔			✔
Tamarind, Tomato and Fennel Sauce (page 41)	✔	✔	✔	✔		
Fennel and Tangerine Vinaigrette (page 42)	✔			✔		
Avocado Chipotle Cream Sauce (page 45)	✔		✔	✔		✔
Pimenton Southern White Sauce (page 46)	✔	✔		✔		
Soursop Sweet and Sour Sauce (page 49)	✔		✔			
Pinot Noir, Cranberry and Roasted Orange Sauce (page 50)	✔					

(continued)

THE SAUCES	POULTRY	MEAT	FISH	VEGETABLES AND PASTA	DESSERTS	DIPPING
Our Never-Fail Go-To Gravy (page 53)	✔					
Persian Pomegranate and Walnut Sauce (Fesanjan) (page 54)	✔					
Everyone's Favorite Tikka Masala Sauce (page 57)	✔		✔	✔		
Dukkah Compound Butter (page 58)	✔					
Szechuan Peppercorn Mignonette (page 63)			✔			
Lemon Verbena Agrodolce (page 64)	✔		✔			
Apricot Sauvignon Blanc Pan Sauce (page 67)	✔		✔			
Umeboshi Plum Vinegar Glaze (page 68)	✔		✔			
Sour Cream and Caramelized Sweet Onion Sauce (page 71)	✔	✔	✔	✔		

THE SAUCES	POULTRY	MEAT	FISH	VEGETABLES AND PASTA	DESSERTS	DIPPING
Rum Lime Glaze (page 72)	✔		✔			
Garlicky Three Chili Clarified Butter Sauce (page 75)	✔		✔			
Roasted Garlic Beurre Blanc (page 76)	✔		✔	✔		✔
Meyer Lemon and Tarragon Beurre Blanc (page 79)			✔	✔		
Miso Brown Butter Sauce (page 80)	✔	✔	✔	✔		
Charif (page 83)			✔			
Saffron and Mace Vinaigrette (page 84)			✔			
Madeira, Black Pepper Allspice Pan Sauce (page 89)		✔				
Spicy Black Tea Jus (page 90)		✔				
Creamy Green Peppercorn Pan Sauce (page 93)		✔				
Red Wine and Fig Pan Sauce (page 94)	✔	✔				

(continued)

THE SAUCES	POULTRY	MEAT	FISH	VEGETABLES AND PASTA	DESSERTS	DIPPING
Grilled Peach and Bourbon Sauce (page 97)	✔	✔				
Slow Roasted Tomato and Cerignola Relish (page 98)	✔	✔	✔			✔
Gochujang and Sake Barbecue Sauce (page 101)	✔	✔				
Pinot Noir and Cassareep Pan Sauce (page 102)		✔				
Burnt Sugar with Scotch Bonnet Steak Sauce (page 105)		✔				
Sour Cherry Chili Sauce (page 106)	✔	✔				
Root Beer Glaze (page 109)		✔				
Coriander and Ginger Glaze (page 110)		✔				
Cuban Mojo (page 113)		✔				
Buccaneer Chimichurri (page 114)	✔	✔	✔			

THE SAUCES	POULTRY	MEAT	FISH	VEGETABLES AND PASTA	DESSERTS	DIPPING
The Ultimate Roast Beef Gravy (page 117)		✔				
Pimento Cheese with Tequila Mornay (page 121)	✔			✔		✔
Broccoli Pesto (page 122)	✔			✔		✔
Caramelized Garlic and Shallot White Wine Sauce (page 125)	✔		✔	✔		
Gorgonzola White Wine Sauce (page 126)	✔			✔		
Curry Butter Sauce (page 129)	✔		✔	✔		
Sage Brown Butter Sauce (page 130)			✔	✔		
Spicy Red Pepper Aioli (page 133)			✔	✔		✔
Coconut Nectar, Pineapple and Thyme Glaze (page 134)	✔			✔		
Grilled Japanese Eggplant and Roasted Tomato Sauce (page 137)				✔		

(continued)

THE SAUCES	POULTRY	MEAT	FISH	VEGETABLES AND PASTA	DESSERTS	DIPPING
Fiddlehead Fern and Garlic Pesto (page 138)				✔		
Roasted Purple Carrot and Ginger Sauce (page 141)				✔		✔
Golden Beet Sauce (page 142)				✔		
Hibiscus Syrup (page 147)					✔	
Extra Dark Mexican Chocolate Sauce (page 148)					✔	
Sweet Almond and Cardamom Cream Sauce (page 151)					✔	
Rum and Orange Glaze (page 152)					✔	
Passion Fruit and Cognac Syrup (page 155)					✔	
Sweet Pickled Ginger (page 156)			✔		✔	
Guava and Ginger Glaze (page 159)					✔	
Candied Rhubarb Sauce (page 160)					✔	

THE SAUCES	POULTRY	MEAT	FISH	VEGETABLES AND PASTA	DESSERTS	DIPPING
Guinness Chocolate Sauce (page 163)					✔	
Salted Coconut Sugar Caramel Sauce (page 164)					✔	
Candied Ginger and Apricot Sauce (page 167)					✔	
Rummy Fruit Compound Butter (page 168)					✔	
Five-Spice and Brown Sugar Compound Butter (page 171)					✔	
Chinese Scallion and Ginger Sauce (page 175)						✔
Tamarind and Date Sauce (page 176)	✔	✔				✔
BasBaas (page 179)	✔		✔			✔
Tropical Fruit Salsa (page 180)	✔	✔	✔			✔
Coconut with Harissa Dipping Sauce (page 183)						✔

SAUCES FOR
Poultry

Poultry—in particular chicken and turkey—have the bad reputation of being dry and flavorless. Of course, this has more to do with the skill of the cook and the method of preparation than the bird itself, but it is true that these are milder in flavor compared to meats like beef, pork, lamb or fish.

The good news is that this makes the most common forms of poultry clean canvases for creative saucing. In fact, just by using a different sauce, simple roast chicken can work for many days of meals, all with a different taste.

Stronger tasting poultry like duck, quail or pheasant hold up well to sauces too, although pairing these requires a bit more finesse to ensure that the flavors don't clash. Darker, more robust poultry like duck, for example, does very well with rich berry notes—whether from wine or from whole fruit itself—something that is also true of pork. Refer to the Sauce Table (page 18) for a chart that shows crossover uses for the sauces in each section.

COCONUT CREAM AND TURMERIC SAUCE

Both coconut and turmeric fall into the realm of newly popular superfoods, and together they are a healthy food powerhouse. We like to use fresh turmeric for this sauce, both for its milder flavor that combines well with the sweetness of the coconut and the white sweet potato (found in Caribbean markets), as well as its deep orange hue.

This complex sauce, redolent with the warmth of ginger and cardamom, can be used two ways—either as a simmering sauce or a spoon-over sauce. To simmer chicken, simply add the chicken pieces to the sauce before reducing it and simmer on medium low heat. You can also make this sauce separately and spoon over chicken or turkey that you have prepared by your favorite dry heat method such as roasting or searing.

MAKES: 1½ cups (360 ml)   **PREP TIME:** 5 minutes   **COOK TIME:** 15 minutes

2 tbsp (30 ml) vegetable or coconut oil

½ cup (121 g) chopped shallots

2 tbsp (29 g) peeled and grated ginger

2 cloves garlic, minced

4 tbsp (34 g) fresh grated turmeric or 2 tbsp (19 g) turmeric powder

¼ tsp ground cinnamon

¼ tsp white pepper

1 cup (240 ml) chicken stock

1 cup (240 ml) coconut milk

Juice of 1 lemon

1 tsp (5 ml) maple syrup

1 cup (180 g) cubed white sweet potato

1 tsp (6 g) salt

¼ tsp cardamom

Heat the oil in a medium saucepan over medium-low heat and add the shallots, ginger and garlic. Sauté for 4 to 5 minutes or until the shallots are softened.

Add the turmeric, cinnamon and white pepper and sauté, stirring, for 30 seconds more.

Pour in the stock and mix well. Add the coconut milk, lemon juice and maple syrup. Mix very well.

Add the sweet potato and reduce heat to a low simmer. Simmer for 15 to 20 minutes or until the sweet potato is fork tender. Season with salt and cardamom and simmer 1 to 2 minutes more.

Pour the sauce into a food processor or high-powered blender and purée until smooth. Return to the pan to reheat if necessary. Add a little more stock, if needed, or reduce for 15 or 20 minutes to achieve a sauce consistency. Serve over pan seared or roast chicken. If using as a simmer sauce, do not reduce and add raw, boneless chicken to the sauce and simmer until done, about 25 to 30 minutes.

SAVORY YUZU AND GINGER SAUCE

Yuzu is an extremely sour Japanese citrus fruit that is most often combined with soy sauce as a dip for fried foods, particularly dumplings. We find that the brightness of the yuzu makes it work well as a pan sauce for seared chicken breasts. This sauce can also be used as a dip for fried chicken wings.

MAKES: ½ cup (120 ml)   **PREP TIME:** 10 minutes   **COOK TIME:** 20 minutes

2 tsp (10 ml) safflower oil

½ shallot, minced

2 tsp (6 g) grated ginger

¼ cup (60 ml) sake

⅓ cup (80 ml) yuzu juice

½ tsp soy sauce

1 cup (240 ml) Chicken Stock (page 13)

¼ tsp white pepper

1 tbsp (15 g) butter

Heat the oil in a small sauté pan over medium heat.

Add the shallot and sauté until translucent, about 2 to 3 minutes. Add the grated ginger and sauté for 1 minute more.

Add the sake and stir well with a wooden spoon, until most of the sake evaporates from the pan and about 1 tablespoon (15 ml) is left, about 2 to 3 minutes.

Add the yuzu juice and soy sauce and simmer until the mixture is reduced by half, about 2 to 3 minutes.

Add the chicken stock and mix well. Simmer for 8 to 9 minutes or until the mixture is reduced by half and the mixture is thick enough to lightly coat the back of a spoon. Season with the white pepper.

Add the butter and stir until melted. Serve as a sauce to accompany chicken or fish or as a dipping sauce for dumplings.

HOISIN HABAÑERO SAUCE

Hoisin is a popular Chinese condiment that can be used on anything from Peking Duck to dumplings. Hoisin is thick, sweet and aromatic thanks to Five-Spice Powder, which combines star anise, Sichuan peppercorns, cinnamon, fennel and cloves. In this stock, we offer a spicy counterpoint to the sweetness of hoisin by combining it with habañero chili pepper brightened up with ginger and rice wine vinegar. The boldness of this sauce makes it good for enlivening barbecued chicken or even used as the flavoring in a chicken and vegetable stir-fry. You can find hoisin sauce in the Asian foods section of most grocery stores.

MAKES: about 1 cup (240 ml)   **PREP TIME:** 10 minutes   **COOK TIME:** 15 minutes

2 tsp (10 ml) safflower oil

2 scallions, end trimmed and white parts sliced thinly

1 tbsp (9 g) peeled, grated ginger

2 cloves garlic, minced

1 whole habañero pepper, pierced

3 tbsp (45 ml) rice wine vinegar

1½ cups (360 ml) Vegetable or Chicken Stock (pages 12 or 13)

½ cup (120 ml) hoisin sauce (available in Asian markets)

¼ cup (60 ml) ketchup

½ tsp salt or to taste

Heat the safflower oil in a small saucepan over medium heat and add the scallions, ginger and garlic. Sauté for 1 to 2 minutes or until the garlic begins to lightly brown.

Add the habañero and sauté for 1 minute. Add the rice wine vinegar and cook for about 30 seconds or until the vinegar is reduced by half.

Stir in the chicken or vegetable stock, hoisin sauce and ketchup. Reduce heat to medium-low and simmer for 10 to 12 minutes or until the mixture is reduced by half. Strain out the habañero pepper. Stir in the salt and adjust, as needed, to taste. Serve with barbecue chicken, dumplings or seared duck breast.

SMOKED TOMATO AND MARCONA ALMOND ROMESCO

Romesco is a classic nut-based Spanish sauce that is most often served with fish, although we find that it is also excellent for poultry, especially for braised chicken thighs that have first been browned until the skin is crispy. While romesco sauces are usually made with pine or hazelnuts, we love the creaminess of marcona almonds—a Spanish almond that is less woody in flavor than more traditional varieties.

Other hallmarks of romesco sauces are roasted tomatoes, red bell peppers and vinegars. Piment d'espelette is a mild, tasty chili pepper largely cultivated in France but which is integral to the Basque cuisine of Northern Spain. We find that it adds a mild spice that enlivens the sauce. You can certainly omit it or substitute another mild pepper if you cannot find piment d'espelette.

MAKES: 2 cups (480 ml)　　**PREP TIME:** 10 minutes　　**COOK TIME:** 30 minutes

3 red bell peppers

½ cup plus 2 tbsp (150 ml) extra virgin olive oil, divided

2 cups (25–30 [300 g]) cherry tomatoes, halved lengthwise

½ cup (72 g) smoked marcona almonds

¼ cup (15 g) chopped flat-leaf parsley

2 cloves garlic, peeled and smashed slightly

3 tbsp (45 ml) sherry vinegar

1 tsp (2 g) smoked paprika

¼ tsp piment d'espelette

Salt and freshly ground black pepper, to taste

Set the oven to broil.

Brush the bell peppers with 1 tablespoon (15 ml) of the olive oil and place them on a tin foiled-lined rimmed sheet pan or in a baking dish. Broil the peppers in the preheated oven until they are blackened and blistered on one side, about 10 minutes. Using tongs, turn over the peppers and broil the other side until blackened and blistered. Remove the peppers from the oven and allow them to cool enough to handle.

Peel the skin from the peppers and remove the stems and seeds. Set aside.

Reduce the oven heat to 400°F (204°C) and lightly brush a rimmed sheet pan with a tablespoon (15 ml) of olive oil. Place the halved cherry tomatoes flat side down and roast them in the oven until they are blistered and beginning to lightly brown, about 20 minutes.

In a food processor, combine the almonds, bell peppers, tomatoes, parsley, garlic and ½ cup (120 ml) of olive oil. Process to make a coarse sauce with some chunks remaining. Add the vinegar, smoked paprika, piment d'espelette and pulse once or twice. Taste the sauce and add salt and black pepper as desired.

Serve over pan-seared fish or chicken. Sauce may be stored, refrigerated, for up to 3 days.

SAVORY CASHEW AND CARDAMOM CREAM SAUCE (KORMA)

Indian food lovers will recognize this simmer sauce as korma, a well flavored and creamy nut-based sauce that can be made with almonds or cashews. Garam masala is the basis for the classic Indian flavor as are the high notes of cardamom, which is almost minty in taste. While you can process your own cashews into a butter or paste very easily, there are so many jarred cashew butters on the market it's often easier to use one of these preparations. We call for cream in this sauce, but it can also be made with coconut cream, and it's just as good. While this sauce is most classically used as a simmer sauce for chunks of boneless chicken, it is also excellent for mixed vegetables or pieces of firm fish like swordfish or catfish too.

MAKES: 2 cups (480 ml)   **PREP TIME:** 15 minutes   **COOK TIME:** 30 minutes

1 tbsp (15 ml) butter

1 small onion, sliced thinly

1 clove garlic, minced

2 tsp (6 g) garam masala

3 green cardamom pods, slightly crushed

½ tsp ground cumin

1½ cups (360 ml) Chicken Stock (page 13) or water

1½ cups (167 g) cashews processed into a paste with ¼ cup (60 ml) water in a food processor or ½ cup (120 ml) almond butter

½ cup (120 ml) heavy cream or coconut cream

½ tsp salt, or more to taste

Freshly ground black pepper to taste

Melt the butter over medium-low heat in a large saucepan and add the onion. Sauté until the onion is golden brown, about 10 minutes.

Add the garlic and sauté 1 minute more, then stir in the garam masala, cardamom pods and cumin. Stir well and sauté for another minute or until the spices release their aromas.

Add the chicken stock or water and the cashew paste and whisk very well until the cashew paste is incorporated. Simmer for 5 minutes, stirring well once or twice more.

Add the heavy cream and salt and simmer 10 minutes more. Season with black pepper to taste.

Pour the sauce into a food processor or a heavy-duty blender and process until completely smooth. Return to the pot to reheat. Add boneless chicken or fish pieces to the sauce and cook until done. You can store the sauce in an airtight jar in the refrigerator for up to 3 days.

HOT HONEY SAUCE

Hot Honey Sauce is a common condiment for fried chicken in parts of the southern United States. Combining the flavors of sweet and spicy, this is a ridiculously easy recipe that brings big flavor. We've used it on deep-fried catfish and chicken-fried steak as well. Using a smoky pepper like chipotle adds a whole new dimension of flavor to this classic. As with any spicy food, the heat level is a matter of personal preference, so feel free to reduce or increase the amount of pepper to your liking.

Many recipes for hot honey sauce call for simply mixing the ingredients together and serving, but we like to heat ours for a short time so that the flavors can truly combine. However, it's important to let the sauce come down to room temperature after cooking so that it will thicken up before using. You can store this sauce in the refrigerator for up to five days, but bring it back to room temperature or gently heat it before using.

MAKES: 1 cup (240 ml)   **PREP TIME:** 5 minutes   **COOK TIME:** 5 minutes

1 cup (240 ml) good quality honey

1 tsp (2 g) powdered chipotle pepper

1 tsp (5 ml) hot sauce of your choice

¼ tsp salt

Combine all the ingredients in a small saucepan over medium heat and whisk well.

Reduce heat to medium-low and simmer for 5 minutes. Remove from the heat and allow to cool to room temperature before using on fried chicken or chicken wings.

TAMARIND, TOMATO AND FENNEL SAUCE

This is an incredibly versatile sauce that we have used for everything from firm white fish, shellfish, chicken or pork, or even as the basis of a stew with chickpeas or on grilled eggplant. This tangy, aromatic sauce that is tempered with a bit of sugar and coconut milk also has some kick thanks to the jalapeño pepper. Feel free to reduce or increase the amount of pepper to your individual taste. The same is true of the sugar in this recipe—you may find you like your sauce a little less tangy so add sweetness accordingly.

MAKES: about 4 cups (960 ml)   **PREP TIME:** 7 minutes   **COOK TIME:** 15 minutes

¼ cup (60 ml) extra virgin olive oil

½ cup (121 g) shallots, sliced

1 red bell pepper, seeded and diced

1 jalapeño pepper, seeded and diced

2 cloves garlic, smashed

1 tbsp (9 g) fresh ginger, peeled and grated

1 tsp (3 g) garam masala

1 tsp (3 g) curry powder

2 tsp (4 g) fennel seeds, toasted and crushed

4 cups (960 ml) drained, canned diced tomatoes

1 tbsp (15 ml) tamarind paste

2 tbsp (13 g) sugar, or to taste

½ cup (120 ml) coconut milk

¼ cup (15 g) chopped cilantro

Salt and pepper to taste

Zest and juice of 1 lime

Heat the olive oil in a medium saucepan over medium heat and add the shallots, bell pepper and jalapeño pepper. Sauté for 2 minutes and add the garlic and ginger. Sauté for 1 minute more.

Stir in the garam masala, curry powder and fennel seeds and sauté 1 minute more.

Add the tomatoes, tamarind paste, sugar and coconut milk. Stir well and lower heat to a simmer. Simmer for 10 to 12 minutes then add the cilantro.

Pour the mixture into a food processor or heavy-duty blender and purée to a smooth sauce. Pour the sauce back into the pot to reheat and add salt and pepper to taste, along with the lime zest and lime juice.

Use immediately as a sauce for pan-seared light meats like chicken or pork or grilled vegetables. Sauce may be stored, refrigerated, in a well sealed container for up to 5 days.

FENNEL AND TANGERINE VINAIGRETTE

We enjoy making this in the winter, when tangerines are at their ripest, and we need a touch of brightness to combat the winter blues. We use this tangy, spicy vinaigrette on salads, grilled mushrooms, roasted beets or over a salad of shaved fennel and arugula.

MAKES: 1 cup (240 ml)   **PREP TIME:** 15 minutes   **COOK TIME:** None

2 tbsp (20 g) finely minced shallot

1 tsp (5 ml) Dijon mustard

1 tsp (2 g) finely grated tangerine zest

2 tbsp (30 ml) fresh tangerine juice

2 tbsp (30 ml) fresh lemon juice

½ tsp ground fennel seed

1 tbsp (4 g) finely chopped fennel fronds, optional

¾ cup (180 ml) extra virgin olive oil

Kosher salt and freshly ground black pepper, to taste

Combine the shallot, mustard, tangerine zest and juice, lemon juice and fennel seed and fronds (if using) in a large bowl and whisk to combine.

Whisking constantly, slowly drizzle in the olive oil. Season with salt and pepper. Serve over sliced chicken breast on a composed salad or roasted root vegetables, or drizzled over roast chicken alone.

AVOCADO CHIPOTLE CREAM SAUCE

Although avocado is mostly used in dips and salads in the United States, it makes its appearance in sauces, soups and even stews in regions where it grows. When gently warmed, this creamy, garlicky sauce with a hint of heat is excellent on grilled chicken or fish, and it is equally good as a condiment for burgers. The sauce may be served cold and do double duty as a dip or salad dressing. You will want to thin the sauce slightly if using warm. If using as a salad dressing, add enough water to achieve an easily pourable consistency and cut the chipotle pepper in half or omit it altogether.

MAKES: about 1 cup (240 ml) **PREP TIME:** 5 to 7 minutes **COOK TIME:** 5 to 10 minutes

½ chipotle chili in sauce (available canned)

1 ripe Haas avocado

1 tbsp (15 ml) plain Greek yogurt

1 clove garlic

½ shallot

Juice of 1 lime

2 tsp (8 g) sugar

1 tbsp (4 g) cilantro leaves

½ tsp salt or to taste

¼ cup (60 ml) water or more as needed

Remove and discard the chipotle stem if it has one.

Place all the ingredients in a high-speed blender or food processor and add water a teaspoon (5 ml) at a time to purée to a smooth, thick but easily pourable sauce.

If using the sauce warm, scrape into a small saucepan and place over a low heat. Bring to just under a boil, stirring often—about 2 to 3 minutes. Serve warm over grilled chicken or fish or as a drizzle over fried chicken tacos.

PIMENTON SOUTHERN WHITE SAUCE

This classic southern barbecue sauce is used as a condiment for grilled food rather than an on-grill flavoring. Easy to make, we use ours on everything from pulled pork sandwiches to roasted potatoes or grilled veggies. Whole grain mustard adds texture and bite to the creamy mayonnaise, which is made piquant by the addition of both garlic and horseradish. It's most delicious on barbecued chicken, and we particularly like to brush finished chicken kebabs with this sauce. You can make this sauce ahead and keep in the refrigerator for up to two weeks.

MAKES: about 1¾ cups (420 ml)   **PREP TIME:** 5 minutes   **COOK TIME:** None

1½ cups (360 ml) mayonnaise

¼ cup (60 ml) white wine vinegar

1 tbsp (9 g) white pepper

1 tbsp (15 ml) whole grain mustard

1 tsp (6 g) salt

1 tsp (2 g) pimenton (smoked paprika)

1 tbsp (14 g) light brown sugar

1 clove garlic, minced

2 tsp (10 ml) prepared horseradish

Whisk all the ingredients together in a medium bowl until well combined. Refrigerate in a tightly sealed container until ready to use. Use as a condiment for barbecue chicken.

SOURSOP SWEET AND SOUR SAUCE

This is an exotic sauce that is simple to make. Soursop is a tropical fruit found in Central and South America and the Caribbean. It has a naturally sweet and sour flavor profile and a milky white consistency when puréed. Called *guanabana* in Spanish, soursop is often used in fruit shakes and ice creams. You can find frozen puréed soursop in the freezer section of Caribbean and Spanish markets or, often, in the Latino foods section of traditional supermarkets. We like to use this sauce as a substitute for traditional Chinese sweet and sour sauces in chicken and vegetable stir-fry.

MAKES: 1 cup (240 ml)

PREP TIME: 5 minutes

COOK TIME: 7 minutes

1 cup (240 ml) soursop purée

Juice of 1 lime

¼ tsp chili pepper flakes

½ tsp garlic powder

¼ tsp salt

2 tsp (5 g) cornstarch dissolved in 2 tsp (10 ml) of water

Combine the soursop, lime juice, chili pepper flakes, garlic powder and salt in a small saucepan over medium heat. Bring to a simmer and simmer for 5 minutes.

Add the cornstarch mixture and whisk well. Bring the mixture to a boil, then reduce to a simmer for 1 to 2 minutes or until the mixture is thick enough to coat the back of a spoon. Use immediately by drizzling over a chicken and vegetable stir-fry or refrigerate in a tightly sealed container for up to 2 weeks.

PINOT NOIR, CRANBERRY AND ROASTED ORANGE SAUCE

This is our alternative to traditional cranberry sauce at Thanksgiving. Orange and cranberry are a match made in culinary heaven and roasting the orange slices adds a caramel flavor that mellows the sauce. We like to sweeten this sauce with honey to temper the tartness of the cranberries. Cara Cara oranges are our favorite because they are delightfully sweet and aromatic. If you can't get Cara Cara oranges, a navel orange will do just fine. A small bit of cayenne pepper adds the slightest bit of heat and dimension to this sauce, but if you don't like it you can omit it.

Cranberries naturally have a lot of pectin, which makes for a lovely thick sauce. We prefer ours chunky but you can certainly purée the finished sauce while it is still hot and then strain through a fine mesh sieve so that the resulting, cooled sauce will actually be a sliceable jelly.

MAKES: 2 cups (480 ml) **PREP TIME:** 10 minutes **COOK TIME:** 1 hour

2 Cara Cara oranges or 1 large navel orange, peeled and most of the white pith removed

Cooking spray, as needed

1 cup plus 2 tbsp (270 ml) honey or more to taste, divided

½ tsp ground cinnamon

10 oz (280 g) fresh or frozen whole cranberries

1 cup (240 ml) water

½ cup (120 ml) pinot noir

1 tsp (6 g) salt

¼ tsp cayenne pepper

2 tbsp (12 g) orange zest

Preheat the oven to 350°F (177°C). Slice the peeled oranges crossways into ¼-inch (6-mm) rounds. Spray a lined baking sheet with cooking spray and arrange the oranges on it, leaving a little space around each round.

Brush the oranges lightly with some of the honey and sprinkle each one lightly with the cinnamon. Bake the orange slices for 30 to 40 minutes or until they are puffy and bubbly, just beginning to turn golden brown. Remove from the oven and cool slightly.

When the orange slices are cool, place in a food processor with the cranberries and pulse into a coarse paste. Scrape this mixture into a medium saucepan with 1 cup (240 ml) of water and the pinot noir.

Place the pan over medium heat and add the remaining honey, salt and cayenne pepper. Simmer this mixture, stirring often, until it is thickened and syrupy, about 30 to 40 minutes. Remove from the heat and stir in the orange zest.

Pour the finished sauce into a bowl and allow to cool to room temperature before serving. The sauce may be refrigerated in a tightly sealed container for up to 2 weeks. Serve with roasted turkey or chicken.

OUR NEVER-FAIL GO-TO GRAVY

Everyone loves a good gravy, yet it seems to be one of those basic preparations that elude many cooks. The key is to approach gravy as a roux-thickened sauce. While pan drippings definitely make for a nice gravy, using chicken stock ensures that the proportions of cooking liquid to fat are easily controlled. For gravies using pan drippings—say from a roast turkey or chicken—use an oil separating cup to remove most of the fat from the drippings or your gravy will be too greasy. Reserve some of the cooking fat to make your roux—about 3 tablespoons (45 ml) worth—and discard the rest. We use a pinch of ground sage, a classic poultry spice, to flavor this poultry gravy along with thyme and celery salt so that the gravy is richly flavored and truly adds pizzazz to the meat. This gravy recipe can be doubled or tripled depending on the size of your bird or your available drippings.

MAKES: 1 cup (240 ml)   **PREP TIME:** 5 minutes   **COOK TIME:** 10 minutes

3 tbsp (45 ml) butter or pan grease from roasted chicken or turkey

2 tbsp (17 g) flour

1½ cups (360 ml) Chicken Stock (page 13) or cooking liquid from roasted chicken or turkey

¼ tsp ground sage

¼ tsp minced thyme leaves

¼ tsp celery salt

¼ tsp white pepper

Salt as needed

Melt the butter or heat the pan grease in a medium saucepan over medium heat.

Add the flour and whisk well until it is completely incorporated into the butter or fat. Continue to cook, whisking, until the flour begins to brown slightly, about 2 minutes.

Add the chicken stock or cooking liquid and whisk well until the mixture is completely combined.

Reduce the heat to a simmer and add the sage, thyme leaves, celery salt and white pepper. Simmer 5 to 6 minutes more or until the mixture is thick enough to coat the back of a spoon. Taste to adjust salt. Serve hot with roast turkey or chicken.

PERSIAN POMEGRANATE AND WALNUT SAUCE (FESANJAN)

This sauce is the basis of the Persian dish Fesanjan that combines the flavors of toasted walnuts and pomegranate in a thick, aromatic sauce for chicken. Traditionally, fesanjan is a special occasion dish and was originally made with wild duck. It is a popular dish for Iranian Jews during Passover. Because this sauce is both hearty and complex in flavor, we find that it's not only good on chicken or duck, but can work well with other game birds like pheasant or quail too. This dish calls for pomegranate juice, which is readily available in most grocery stores, but also pomegranate molasses, which can be called pomegranate syrup. This is available in Middle Eastern grocery stores and is a necessary ingredient that shouldn't be omitted.

MAKES: about 2 cups (480 ml) **PREP TIME:** 15 minutes **COOK TIME:** 30 to 40 minutes

½ tsp saffron powder

⅓ cup (30 ml) boiling water

1 cup (110 g) walnuts, ground to a fine powder

1 tbsp (15 g) butter

1 small onion, minced

1 cup (240 ml) Chicken Stock (page 13)

½ cup (120 ml) pomegranate juice

¼ cup (60 ml) pomegranate molasses or syrup

¼ cup (50 g) sugar, or more to taste

1 tsp (6 g) salt, or more to taste

Dissolve the saffron powder in ⅓ cup (80 ml) boiling water and set aside.

Toast the ground walnuts in a medium frying pan over medium heat, stirring often, until the nuts are deep golden brown in color, about 3 to 5 minutes. Remove from the heat and set aside.

Melt the butter in a medium saucepan over medium heat and then add the onion. Sauté the onion until softened, about 8 to 9 minutes and then add the toasted walnut powder and mix well.

Stir in the chicken stock, pomegranate juice, pomegranate molasses and sugar. Mix well and lower the heat to simmer. Simmer for 15 minutes, uncovered.

Add the saffron liquid and salt. Simmer 15 minutes more or until the sauce is reduced by a third and is thick like a mole. The sauce can be used by adding boneless chicken pieces to it in the last 20 minutes of cooking or by spooning the finished sauce over roasted chicken or turkey.

EVERYONE'S FAVORITE TIKKA MASALA SAUCE

Chicken Tikka Masala is probably the best known of all Indian restaurant dishes and one of the most beloved. A secret about this creamy tomato-flavored sauce: It's not a traditional Indian dish at all. Tikka masala was created in a London restaurant by an Indian chef who wanted to meld in South Asian flavors with western sauce ingredients in order to appeal to English audiences. The end result is this sauce that features both garam masala and ginger and tomato paste and heavy cream.

This is a great simmer sauce to make ahead and keep in the refrigerator for a quick Indian-inspired meal. It's equally good with chickpeas, lentils, boneless chicken, fish or shrimp. Simply cook your main ingredient, and then add it to the tikka masala sauce and simmer together for 20 minutes to combine the flavors. One of our favorite, easy preparations is to cube chicken breast and season them with garam masala, ginger and tandoori seasoning, which is now widely available in the spice aisle of grocery stores. We bake the pieces in the oven or grill them and add to the tikka masala sauce. Fenugreek leaves add an authentic flavor to this dish but if you can't find it feel free to omit or simply garnish your finished dish with parsley or cilantro leaves.

MAKES: about 2 cups (480 ml)   **PREP TIME:** 5 minutes   **COOK TIME:** 15 minutes

2 tbsp (30 g) butter

1 tbsp (9 g) garam masala

1 tbsp (9 g) tandoori seasoning

½ tsp ground ginger

2 tbsp (30 ml) tomato paste

1½ cups (360 ml) Chicken Stock (page 13)

1½ cups (360 ml) heavy cream

1 tsp (6 g) salt or more to taste

2 tsp (1 g) dried fenugreek leaves, optional

Melt the butter in a medium saucepan over medium low heat and add the garam masala, tandoori seasoning and ground ginger. Cook for 1 minute, stirring well.

Add the tomato paste and cook, stirring, 1 more minute.

Pour in the chicken stock and use a whisk to stir well and break up lumps. Simmer for 1 to 2 minutes, then add the heavy cream and salt. Whisk well, until smooth, and reduce the heat to medium-low. Simmer for 10 minutes.

If using, rub the fenugreek leaves into a powder between your palms and add to the sauce. Simmer for an additional 5 minutes. Add cooked chicken, fish, lentils or shrimp and simmer on the lowest heat setting for 20 minutes. Alternatively, store the finished sauce in a tightly sealed container in your refrigerator to use within 3 days.

DUKKAH COMPOUND BUTTER

We love compound butters because they are a versatile way to add flavor to existing sauces, serve as a flavorful condiment or topping or, melted, become a sauce in themselves.

This version makes use of dukkah, a tangy, woody Egyptian seasoning mixture that is made of toasted nuts, herbs and spices and is used to flavor proteins or served with olive oil as a dip for pita bread. Here we've mixed dukkah with softened butter that is then re-chilled. It is ideal for a quick sauce for meats or even vegetables but one of our favorite uses is to melt the Dukkah Compound Butter and use it to baste sunny-side up eggs to complete their cooking while infusing flavor.

MAKES: ½ cup (120 g)   **PREP TIME:** 2 minutes   **COOK TIME:** 2 minutes

8 tbsp (120 g) unsalted butter, softened

2 tbsp (9 g) Dukkah

In a small bowl, mix the butter and dukkah together until well combined.

Scrape the flavored butter into a small dish and cover well with plastic wrap. Refrigerate until the butter is hard, about 8 hours. Use slices on top of grilled or pan seared poultry and meat or melted to finish sunny-side up eggs.

SAUCES FOR
Fish

Sauces are the mainstay of classic French cuisine and no protein got the saucy treatment more than fish. Cream sauces and butter sauces, in particular, were used to drown seafood so their natural flavors didn't come through.

Happily, with modern cuisine and the availability of very fresh seafood nearly anywhere in the country, there is no longer the need to smother your fish in order to eat it. Instead, the seafood sauces we have created here use the bright flavors of herbs, citrus and spices to enhance the flavors of both shellfish and fin fish.

Of course, classic flavors of butter and cream do make an appearance because who doesn't like a delicate piece of fish kissed with the flavor of butter?

SZECHUAN PEPPERCORN MIGNONETTE

Mignonette is a classic sauce served with raw oysters, although we find it can be an excellent dipping sauce for fried oysters as well. It's also great on raw clams on the half shell. Mignonettes always feature shallots or onions, peppercorns and vinegar. Our version calls for pink Szechuan peppercorns—a spicier peppercorn than black, white or green varieties, scallions and rice wine vinegar. You can keep mignonettes for quite a few weeks in the refrigerator—it won't go bad, but the pepper flavor will get more intense, so keep that in mind.

MAKES: ½ cup (120 ml)   **PREP TIME:** 5 minutes   **COOK TIME:** None

2 tbsp (26 g) Szechuan peppercorns

2 tbsp (6 g) scallions, white part only, minced

½ cup (60 ml) rice wine vinegar

¼ tsp Himalayan pink salt, or to taste

Whisk all the ingredients together in a small bowl and refrigerate in a sealed container until ready to use. Serve 1 teaspoon (5 ml) of sauce on raw, chilled oysters.

LEMON VERBENA AGRODOLCE

Argrodolce translates to sour and sweet in Italian and is a deliciously sticky, tangy and sweet sauce with multiple purposes. This sauce could also be called a gastrique if using the French term. Combining sugar and honey with vinegar and other flavorings, agrodolces can be on the lighter side as in this version for a hearty fish such as a swordfish steak or plummy with raisins and dried fruit, which makes a lovely condiment for sandwiches.

Here we use lemon verbena, a delicate herb with a lightly sweet lemon aroma, along with lemon juice and zest. The lemon verbena leaves are used whole to showcase their lovely oblong shape. Champagne vinegar adds a sophisticated tang to the sauce, which is even light enough for a more delicate fish like flounder.

MAKES: ½ cup (120 ml)   **PREP TIME:** 10 minutes   **COOK TIME:** 45 minutes

1 tbsp (15 ml) pistachio oil

3 tbsp (45 g) minced shallots

1¾ cups (420 ml) champagne vinegar

¼ cup (60 ml) freshly squeezed lemon juice

⅓ cup (67 g) sugar

¼ tsp white pepper

¼ tsp salt

Zest of one lemon

10 small lemon verbena leaves

Heat the pistachio oil in a medium saucepan over medium heat and add the shallots. Sauté the shallots until they are translucent, about 2 to 3 minutes.

Add the champagne vinegar, lemon juice, sugar, white pepper and salt. Whisk well then reduce the heat to a simmer and simmer until the mixture is thick and syrupy and reduced by roughly half, about 40 to 45 minutes.

Stir in the lemon zest and the verbena leaves and mix well. Serve hot over pan-seared fillet of white fish.

APRICOT SAUVIGNON BLANC PAN SAUCE

This fruity pan sauce offers a bright alternative to a simple spritz of lemon or lime on fish. It works equally well on fish fillets or as a dipping sauce for shrimp, crab or lobster. Apricot juice is readily found in most supermarkets but we find that Santa Cruz Organic is a widely available brand with excellent flavor and consistency. Sauvignon Blanc is the wine we choose for this sauce because of its clean, acid composition. The New Zealand sauvignons are among our favorites. This sauce works well with pan-seared chicken breasts as well, in which case, you can use the same pan in which you seared the chicken to make the sauce.

MAKES: ½ cup (120 ml)   **PREP TIME:** 5 minutes   **COOK TIME:** 20 minutes

1 tbsp (15 ml) safflower oil

1 small shallot, minced

¼ tsp minced thyme

½ cup (120 ml) sauvignon blanc

¾ cup (180 ml) Chicken Stock (page 13)

⅓ cup (80 ml) apricot juice

2 tsp (10 ml) apricot preserves

½ tsp white pepper

½ tsp salt

1 tbsp (15 g) European style butter

Heat the safflower oil in a medium sauté pan over medium heat and add the shallot. Sauté the shallot until softened and clear, about 2 to 3 minutes. Add the thyme and sauté 1 minute more.

Add the sauvignon blanc and reduce the heat to a simmer. Simmer until the wine is almost entirely evaporated, about 5 to 6 minutes.

Add the chicken stock and apricot juice, apricot preserves, white pepper and salt. Whisk well to dissolve the preserves and continue to simmer the mixture until bubbles spread evenly across the pan and the mixture can coat the back of a spoon without dripping, about 5 to 7 minutes. Stir in the butter until it's melted. Serve hot over baked flounder or halibut or use as a dipping sauce for lobster or crab legs.

UMEBOSHI PLUM VINEGAR GLAZE

This glaze makes use of umeboshi or ume plums, a small Japanese plum that is usually pickled whole or processed into a paste. The spiciness of fresh ginger and sake round out this unique glaze that is particularly ideal for oily and fatty fish such as salmon or sardines. As with any wine or liquor used in cooking, use the best quality sake you can find to deglaze the pan in this recipe—ideally one that would traditionally be consumed hot rather than cold.

MAKES: 1 cup (240 ml)　　**PREP TIME:** 10 minutes　　**COOK TIME:** 20 minutes

1 tbsp (15 ml) safflower oil

½ shallot, minced

1 tbsp (9 g) grated fresh ginger

¼ cup (60 ml) sake

¼ cup (60 ml) ume plum vinegar

1 cup (240 ml) Chicken Stock (page 13)

3 tbsp (45 ml) umeboshi plum paste

¼ tsp white pepper

⅛ tsp star anise powder

¼ tsp salt or to taste

1 tbsp (15 g) European style butter

Heat the safflower oil in a medium sauté pan over medium heat and add the shallot. Sauté the shallot until softened and clear, about 2 to 3 minutes. Add the grated ginger and sauté 1 minute more.

Add the sake and the ume plum vinegar and stir well. Reduce the heat to a simmer and simmer until almost evaporated, about 5 to 6 minutes.

Add the chicken stock, umeboshi plum paste, white pepper, star anise powder and salt and whisk well.

Simmer the mixture until bubbles spread evenly across the pan and the mixture can coat the back of a spoon without dripping, about 8 to 9 minutes. Stir in the butter until it's melted. Brush over grilled salmon.

SOUR CREAM AND CARAMELIZED SWEET ONION SAUCE

Consider this sauce the sophisticated version of classic sour cream and onion dip. Featuring caramelized onions, the sauce is both sweet and creamy with a hint of umami—meatiness. It can be used cold as a topper for crudités or chips, but heated up with a little heavy cream it is an ideal sauce for grilled chicken breasts, pork chops or baked potatoes. It is also an excellent cold sauce for a composed salad. Use any variety of sweet onion such as Vidalia, Walla Walla or Maui Sweets for the best results.

MAKES: 1½ to 2 cups (360 to 480 ml)   **PREP TIME:** 5 minutes   **COOK TIME:** 12 to 15 minutes

1 tbsp (15 g) unsalted butter

1 tsp (5 ml) safflower oil

1 small sweet onion, thinly sliced

2 cloves garlic, whole

Salt and freshly ground pepper to taste

½ tsp fresh thyme leaves

1½ cups (360 ml) sour cream

½ cup (120 ml) heavy cream (optional, for warm sauce)

Heat the butter and oil in a medium frying pan over medium-low heat until the butter melts.

Add the onion and fry for 2 to 3 minutes. Add the garlic and reduce the heat to low and continue to fry until the onion is deeply golden brown and soft, about 7 to 8 minutes.

Season with salt, freshly ground pepper to taste and the thyme leaves. Fry for 1 minute more. Remove the onion from the heat and allow it to cool completely.

Scrape the onion and garlic into the bowl of a food processor or blender and pulse a few times into a coarse paste.

In a medium bowl, mix together the onion and sour cream and serve cold as a dip for crudités or chips. To use as a warm sauce, place the sour cream mixture in a small saucepan with the heavy cream over low heat. Heat the sauce for 1 to 2 minutes, whisking well the whole time. Serve warm over fish, meats or steamed vegetables.

RUM LIME GLAZE

The classic Caribbean pairings of rum and lime are often used with fish and for good reason. The citrus freshness of the lime and the aromatic sweetness of the rum are naturally good together. We find that this is an ideal glaze for grilled fish whether they are whole, fillets or chunks as for kebabs. This is a particularly good glaze for grilled shrimp or scallops.

MAKES: about ½ cup (120 ml) **PREP TIME:** 5 minutes **COOK TIME:** 10 minutes

1 tbsp (15 ml) safflower oil

½ shallot, minced

¼ cup (60 ml) spiced rum

Juice of 1 lime

1 cup (240 ml) Chicken Stock (page 13)

1 tbsp (14 g) brown sugar

¼ tsp chili powder, or to taste

⅛ tsp ground allspice

1 tbsp (15 g) European style butter

Heat the safflower oil in a medium sauté pan over medium heat and add the shallot. Fry the shallot until it's softened and clear, about 2 to 3 minutes.

Add the rum and the lime juice and reduce the heat to a simmer. Simmer until the mixture is almost evaporated, 9 to 10 minutes.

Pour in the chicken stock and add the brown sugar, chili powder and allspice. Simmer the mixture until bubbles spread evenly across the pan and the mixture can coat the back of a spoon without dripping, about 8 to 10 minutes. Stir in the butter until melted. Serve hot over a thick cut of fish steak that has been grilled or pan seared.

GARLICKY THREE CHILI CLARIFIED BUTTER SAUCE

This clarified butter sauce, traditionally used with seafood, features three types of dried chilies, each chosen for their specific flavors. Chile de arbol is a bright red, extremely hot pepper that adds color and spice. Chipotle pepper adds smoke and the ancho chili is milder in heat and deeper in color. The chilies are gently fried in butter as it is clarified, then removed before serving.

The clarification process—cooking butter over low heat so the milk solids cook out—makes a perfectly clear dipping sauce with nutty undertones. This sauce is a spicy one, so it's ideal for heartier fish rather than a delicate sole or flounder and is a delicious dipping sauce for steamed lobster, crab or clams.

MAKES: about 1 cup (240 ml) **PREP TIME:** 30 minutes **COOK TIME:** 20 to 25 minutes

16 tbsp (240 g) salted European style butter

1 chile de arbol

1 ancho chili

¼ tsp dried chipotle pepper

5 cloves garlic

½ tsp salt or to taste

Melt the butter in a small saucepan over medium heat. When all the butter is melted, reduce the heat to low and add the chilies and garlic.

Continue to cook the butter on a low simmer. It will foam up and then die down. Let the butter simmer for about 20 minutes or until you see a whitish residue at the bottom of your pan. These are the milk solids. Keep an eye on your garlic—do not let it burn. Pick out the garlic when it is deeply brown.

Remove the chilies with a slotted spoon and pour the butter into a bowl through a fine mesh sieve to strain out the milk solids. Season with salt to taste. Serve hot as a dipping sauce for steamed clams, lobster or crab legs. The butter may be refrigerated and melted again before use.

ROASTED GARLIC BEURRE BLANC

Beurre Blanc is a traditional French mild and creamy emulsified sauce served hot like Hollandaise. It is velvety and rich and is a wonderful canvas upon which to build layers of flavor using herbs and seasoning. Unlike Hollandaise, it does not have egg yolks, and unlike cold emulsifications like mayonnaise, it is thick and coats foods nicely without being spreadable. Beurre blanc translates to white butter, which is the main ingredient in the sauce. When making Beurre Blanc, use very cold butter, as that is a key aspect of making the emulsification work. Another trick to ensure that your sauce doesn't break is to cook it over a very low heat, and absolutely do not let it come to a boil.

If, however, your sauce breaks or does not come together, you can use a small amount of cream to bind it. We offer two versions of Beurre Blanc in this book—this one, which uses vinegar as is traditional but substitutes the sweetness of roasted garlic for the customary shallots, and another that makes use of Meyer lemon and tarragon (page 79).

MAKES: 1½ cups (360 ml) **PREP TIME:** 10 minutes **COOK TIME:** 1 hour 15 minutes

1 head garlic

1 tbsp (15 ml) olive oil

¼ cup (60 ml) white wine vinegar

¼ cup (60 ml) very dry white wine

24 tbsp (360 g) cold butter, cut into tablespoon-size (15-g) chunks

½ tsp salt or more to taste

¼ tsp white pepper

2 tsp (10 ml) fresh squeezed lemon juice

Preheat the oven to 400°F (204°C).

Holding the garlic head sideways, trim ¼ inch (6 mm) off the top. Set the garlic on a piece of tin foil that is large enough to enfold it. Drizzle the garlic with the olive oil and wrap it in the foil. Bake for 1 hour or until the garlic is browned and can be pierced easily with a fork. Remove from the oven and cool.

Peel 8 to 10 cloves of the roasted garlic and mash lightly with a fork. Combine this in a medium saucepan over medium heat along with the wine vinegar and wine. Whisk well to combine.

Boil this mixture until almost all of the liquid is reduced, about 10 minutes. You should have about 2 tablespoons (30 ml) of the garlic mixture left.

Reduce the heat to its lowest setting and add 1 tablespoon (15 g) of butter and whisk until it melts. Continue with the remaining pieces of butter, whisking each piece until it melts before adding the next piece. This will take roughly 15 minutes.

Once all the butter is incorporated, add the salt, pepper and lemon juice and whisk again to combine. Serve over breaded, fried fish fillets such as rainbow trout.

MEYER LEMON AND TARRAGON BEURRE BLANC

This version of Beurre Blanc, the classic French white sauce, is more traditional in its use of shallots but forgoes vinegar for the aromatic and balanced tartness of Meyer lemon juice. We use Meyer lemon zest to finish the sauce at the end as well. If you cannot find Meyer lemons, then by all means substitute regular lemon juice—as long as it is fresh and not from a bottle. Tarragon is an herb that works particularly well with lemon and white wine, and we find that this simple sauce really elevates mild fish like sole, flounder or fluke.

MAKES: 1½ cups (360 ml)   **PREP TIME:** 10 minutes   **COOK TIME:** 20 minutes

1 shallot, finely minced

1 tbsp (4 g) finely minced tarragon

¼ cup (60 ml) freshly squeezed Meyer lemon juice

¼ cup (60 ml) very dry white wine

24 tbsp (360 g) cold butter, cut into tablespoon-size (15-g) chunks

¼ tsp salt or more to taste

¼ tsp white pepper

1 tsp (5 ml) Meyer lemon zest

Combine the shallot, tarragon, Meyer lemon juice and white wine in a medium saucepan over medium heat.

Boil this mixture until almost all of the liquid is reduced, about 10 minutes. You should have about 1½ tablespoons (22 ml) of liquid left.

Reduce heat to its lowest setting and add 1 tablespoon (15 g) of butter and whisk until it melts. Continue with the remaining pieces of butter, whisking each piece until it melts before adding the next piece. This will take you about 15 minutes.

Once all the butter is incorporated, add the salt, pepper and lemon zest and whisk again to combine. Serve over mild fish or pan seared scallops.

MISO BROWN BUTTER SAUCE

Caramelized butter combined with the umami saltiness of white miso makes this a robust sauce that goes well with pork, chicken, roasted vegetables and even pasta. This recipe calls for white miso, which has the mildest color and flavor, making it easier to pair with other sauce ingredients without overwhelming the final product. There are only three ingredients in this simple but delicious sauce, but the fourth is patience. The trick for an excellent final result is that the butter be browned slowly, allowing the milk solids to caramelize. Raise the heat too high or leave the pan unattended and you run the risk of scorching the butter for a burned and unpalatable mess.

MAKES: about ½ cup (120 ml)   **PREP TIME:** 2 minutes   **COOK TIME:** 12 to 15 minutes

8 tbsp (120 g) unsalted butter, cut into tablespoon-size (15-g) chunks

1 tbsp (15 ml) white miso

Freshly ground white pepper, to taste

Place all the butter pieces evenly in a medium skillet set over low heat.

When the butter pieces begin to melt, gently stir them with a rubber spatula or wooden spoon. Keep stirring vigorously while the butter is cooking and continues to bubble and brown, about 10 to 11 minutes.

Once the butter is about the color of light brown sugar, pour the mixture out of a pan through a fine mesh sieve into a waiting bowl—the butter will continue to brown for a time after it is removed from the hot pan. Whisk in the miso paste until it is totally combined and season with the white pepper. Strain the sauce through a fine mesh strainer—it will be lumpy. Serve hot over breaded, baked bay scallops of your choice or toss with pasta or grilled or roasted vegetables.

CHARIF

Charif is a spicy sauce attributed to North African Jewish cuisine. Essentially a purée of various ingredients in a tomato base, charif serves triple duty as a condiment, a seasoning paste for meats or, when watered down, a cooking sauce for fish. Our version ups the traditional amount of tomatoes for a more sauce-like consistency. We like to use jarred red hot cherry peppers for this sauce as well as a dash of Aleppo pepper—a hot pepper flake originally from Syria, because we feel the sweetness of the cherry pepper and the fruity, cumin-like notes from the Aleppo pepper make for a more complex sauce. Although this fast sauce can be used immediately, refrigerating the sauce at least overnight allows the flavor to develop further, so do so if you can.

MAKES: about 3 cups (720 ml)   **PREP TIME:** 5 minutes   **COOK TIME:** 15 minutes

1 red bell pepper

¼ cup (60 ml) extra virgin olive oil, divided

4 cloves garlic

4 red hot cherry peppers, stemmed and seeded

½ tsp Aleppo pepper flakes

⅓ cup (80 ml) white wine vinegar

1 (28-oz [828-ml]) can whole tomatoes, drained

2 tsp (10 g) coarse salt

1½ tsp (5 g) ground cumin

½ tsp ground coriander

Preheat the oven to broil. Brush the bell pepper with olive oil and place it on a tin foiled lined rimmed sheet pan or in a baking dish. Broil the pepper in the preheated oven until it's blackened and blistered on one side, about 7 to 8 minutes. Using tongs, turn over the pepper and roast the other side until blackened and blistered, another 7 to 8 minutes. Remove the pepper from the oven and allow it to cool enough to handle. Peel the skin from the peppers and remove the stems and seeds.

Place the red bell pepper and the remaining olive oil, garlic, cherry peppers, pepper flakes, vinegar, tomatoes, salt, cumin and coriander in the bowl of a food processor and pulse to a thick sauce, about 1 minute.

Scrape the sauce into an airtight container and refrigerate. Pour, as desired, over fish pieces to stew or over whole, deep-fried fish such as larger sardines or red mullet.

SAFFRON AND MACE VINAIGRETTE

We tend to think of vinaigrette as salad dressing but this quick sauce has a wide variety of potential uses from a marinade for meats and fish to a dip for crudités. This version uses saffron, which adds bold color and a delicate aroma and taste. Mace is a somewhat astringent spice that comes from the membrane surrounding a nutmeg, and it complements saffron's flavor nicely.

This vinaigrette is good spooned over any firm fleshed white fish and is delightful on steamed vegetables too. Whenever we make vinaigrettes we like to macerate the herbs and aromatics in the vinegar for a short time before adding the oil; this allows their full flavor to imbue the vinegar and, ultimately, the completed vinaigrette.

MAKES: about 1½ cups (360 ml)   **PREP TIME:** 15 minutes   **COOK TIME:** None

¼ tsp ground saffron

1 tbsp (15 ml) boiling water

½ tsp sugar

⅓ cup (80 ml) champagne vinegar

½ shallot, minced

½ tsp minced thyme leaves

¼ tsp salt, or to taste

Freshly ground black pepper to taste

⅛ tsp ground mace

1 cup (240 ml) extra virgin olive oil

Dissolve the saffron in 1 tablespoon (15 ml) of boiling water and set aside for the color to deepen and the water to cool.

Combine the sugar and vinegar in a medium bowl and whisk well so that the sugar dissolves. Add the shallot and thyme and set aside for 10 minutes.

Stir in the saffron water, salt, pepper and mace.

Pour the olive oil into the vinegar mixture in a thin stream while whisking vigorously until all the olive oil is used up. Use immediately over steamed vegetables or grilled white Alaskan salmon and store in a sealed container for up to 2 days. Shake the vinaigrette well to use if it has been sitting.

SAUCES FOR
Meat

Here you will find some of the more robust sauces in the book. Developed for use with beef, pork and lamb, many of these sauces like Red Wine Fig (page 94) or Caribbean Buccaneer Chimichurri (page 114) would be excellent for use on game such as venison, wild boar or elk as well.

The pan-sauce technique is featured prominently in this chapter because it remains one of the best sauce methods for meats—particularly those that are pan seared or pan roasted, giving up that delicious fond that can be used to add flavor and complexity to the sauce.

Once you've mastered the pan sauce technique, we're sure you'll want to use it more and more, and we encourage you to experiment with different aromatics and deglazing liquids to come up with your own unique recipes.

MADEIRA, BLACK PEPPER AND ALLSPICE PAN SAUCE

Madeira is a fortified wine made on Madeira Island of Portugal. Once a key part of American culture—Thomas Jefferson and George Washington were fans, as were most of their social contemporaries—now Madeira is virtually unknown to American drinkers. Produced in varying levels of dryness from dry to sweet, Madeira has high acidity levels, which makes it a perfect base for sauces to accompany fatty proteins. We particularly like to use it with pork, and this easy pan sauce has just a hint of sweetness with a clean acidic finish that goes excellently with pan-fried pork chops. Use the drippings from cooking the pork chops in place of safflower oil if you can. In fact, you can make the sauce in the same pan once the pork chops are removed. The easiest way to crack the peppercorns for this sauce is using a mortar and pestle.

MAKES: ¼ cup (60 ml)   **PREP TIME:** 10 minutes   **COOK TIME:** 15 minutes

2 tsp (10 ml) safflower oil

1 shallot, minced finely

½ tsp minced thyme leaves

1 tsp (5 g) cracked black peppercorns

¼ cup (60 ml) medium-sweet Madeira

1 tsp (5 ml) freshly squeezed lemon juice

1 cup (240 ml) Meat Stock (page 14)

¼ tsp salt

¼ tsp freshly ground pepper

⅛ tsp allspice

1 tbsp (15 g) cold butter

Heat the safflower oil in a small sauté pan over medium low heat and add the shallot, thyme and peppercorns. Sauté until the shallot is softened, about 2 to 3 minutes.

Add the Madeira and lemon juice and simmer until the liquid is reduced by a little less than half, about 3 to 4 minutes.

Add the meat stock and whisk well. Simmer the sauce until bubbles form across the entire pan and the liquid is reduced by half, about 8 minutes.

Stir in the salt, pepper and allspice. Remove the pan from heat and add the butter and stir until it is melted. Serve spooned over pork chops.

SPICY BLACK TEA JUS

Jus or juice is a sauce that is not as thick as gravy or pan sauce but thicker than broth. It is often referred to as a light gravy. Here we add the flavor of black tea—we like to use Earl Grey for the bergamot flavor, which is slightly flowery, but you can use any dark tea that suits you—just be sure it isn't fruit or heavy spice flavored. Here we are using Shiraz wine with its rich berry undertones but any full-bodied red wine will work too. Use this jus with filet mignon, roast beef or beef tenderloin medallions.

MAKES: 1 cup (240 ml) **PREP TIME:** 10 minutes **COOK TIME:** 40 minutes

1½ cups (360 ml) Meat Stock (page 14)

2 Earl Grey tea bags

1 tbsp (15 ml) safflower oil

2 tbsp (30 g) minced shallots

1 small Thai red chili pepper, pierced

½ cup (120 ml) Shiraz wine

⅛ tsp nutmeg

Salt and pepper to taste

Heat the meat stock in a medium saucepan until it just simmers, about 4 to 5 minutes, and add the tea bags. Cover and set aside to steep for 15 minutes. Remove the tea bags and discard.

Heat the safflower oil in another medium saucepan over medium heat and add the shallots. Sauté until the shallots are softened, about 2 to 3 minutes. Add the Thai chili pepper and sauté 1 minute more.

Pour in the steeped stock and wine and mix well. Add the nutmeg and simmer this mixture until it is reduced by a little less than half, about 25 to 30 minutes. The mixture should loosely coat the back of a spoon but still be able to drip off.

Strain through a fine mesh strainer and season with salt and pepper to taste. Serve hot spooned over filet mignon or sliced beef tenderloin medallions.

CREAMY GREEN PEPPERCORN PAN SAUCE

This classic French pan sauce for thick boneless steaks like filet mignon is not seen much anymore, and that's a pity because it's a truly superb accompaniment to a well seared cut of tender beef. Tangy, slightly spicy and creamy, the sauce is also aromatic thanks to the kiss of brandy. As with all pan sauces, this one will taste best if it is made in the same pan used to sear the fillet— so that it can be enriched by the fond.

If you are using the same pan, only add the additional oil as is necessary. However, filet mignon and similar cuts are not particularly fatty so you'll likely need to use the amount of oil as we suggest here.

MAKES: about ½ cup (120 ml)   **PREP TIME:** 5 minutes   **COOK TIME:** 10 to 12 minutes

2 tsp (10 ml) safflower oil

1 shallot, finely minced

2 tsp (5 g) brined green peppercorns, drained

¼ cup (60 ml) brandy

1 cup (240 ml) Meat Stock (page 14)

½ cup (120 ml) heavy cream

½ tsp salt

1 tbsp (15 g) cold butter

Heat the safflower oil in a small sauté pan over medium-low heat and add the shallot. Sauté until the shallot is softened, about 2 to 3 minutes. Add the peppercorns and sauté for 1 minute more.

Add the brandy and simmer until the liquid is reduced and about 1 tablespoon (15 ml) remains, about 1 minute.

Add the beef stock and whisk well. Simmer the sauce until bubbles form across the entire pan and the liquid is reduced by half, about 8 to 10 minutes.

Stir in the heavy cream and salt and simmer until the sauce is thickened and can coat the back of a spoon without dripping, about 2 to 3 minutes. Whisk in the butter until it is melted. Serve hot over a thick porterhouse or other aged steak.

RED WINE AND FIG PAN SAUCE

This combination of figs and full-bodied red wine is also prepared using the classic method for pan sauce. Because of its sweeter, jammier flavor profile, this is an ideal sauce for pork chops, pork loin, tender cuts of beef or even turkey, which are often served with jammy compotes, or sauces. It's important to use a rich wine such as a zinfandel.

If you are preparing your meat using a pan-seared or roasting method, then use the fat drippings to replace the oil called for in step one. A tip when making any wine-based sauce—use the wine you'd want to drink. Lesser quality wines make lesser quality sauces. A pat of butter is added once the sauce is completed to add creaminess and a high gloss. This traditional finishing step is called *monter au beurre* or "mounting with butter" and adds a velvety sheen and texture to the sauce.

MAKES: about ½ cup (120 ml)   **PREP TIME:** 5 minutes   **COOK TIME:** 8 to 10 minutes

---

1 tbsp (15 ml) pistachio oil or pan drippings

½ shallot, minced

1 tsp (2 g) minced thyme leaves

½ cup (120 ml) good quality zinfandel, merlot or Rioja

1 cup (240 ml) Meat Stock (page 14) or veal stock

1 tbsp (15 ml) fig jam

Salt and pepper to taste

1 tbsp (15 g) butter

Heat a medium frying pan over medium-low heat and add the pistachio oil or pan drippings. Add the shallot and thyme leaves and sauté until the shallot begins to soften, about 2 to 3 minutes.

Pour in the wine. Simmer the mixture until it is reduced by half, about 5 to 6 minutes.

Add the stock to the pan and continue to simmer until the mixture reduces by about two-thirds or until there are bubbles across the entire surface of the pan. Add the fig jam, whisk well to combine and simmer 30 seconds more.

Test the consistency of the sauce by dipping the back of a spoon in the sauce and running one finger through the middle of the spoon to form a channel. If the sauce doesn't ooze back across the area you swiped, then it is at the nappé stage and is ready. Season with salt and pepper to taste.

Stir the butter into the pan until it melts. Serve 2 to 3 tablespoons (30 to 45 ml) of sauce per serving of sliced roast beef or prime rib of beef.

GRILLED PEACH AND BOURBON SAUCE

Fruit sauces like this one and the Sour Cherry Chili Sauce (page 106) work wonderfully well with pork. The sweet and smoky flavor of a grilled peach is an ideal complement to the smokiness of a good quality bourbon. Ginger adds a bit of heat without spice. Serve this with pork chops, pork kebabs or even use as a glaze for ham.

MAKES: about ½ cup (120 ml)   **PREP TIME:** 10 minutes   **COOK TIME:** 30 minutes

1 ripe peach, halved and pit removed

1 tbsp (15 ml) safflower oil, plus more as needed, divided

½ shallot, minced

1 tsp (3 g) grated fresh ginger

½ cup (120 ml) bourbon

1 cup (240 ml) Chicken Stock (page 13)

¼ tsp white pepper

⅛ tsp allspice

¼ tsp salt or to taste

1 tbsp (15 g) European style butter

Preheat the grill to high and brush the two peach halves with safflower oil. Grill, away from the direct heat, flesh side down, for 3 to 8 minutes, then turn over and grill skin side down for 1 to 2 minutes. Remove the peach halves from the grill and then allow them to cool. When they are cool enough to handle, purée in a heavy-duty food processor or blender. Strain the purée through a fine mesh sieve to remove any pieces of skin. Set aside.

Heat the safflower oil in a medium sauté pan over medium heat and add the shallot. Fry the shallot until it's softened and clear, about 1 to 2 minutes. Add the grated ginger and fry 1 minute more.

Add the bourbon and stir well. Reduce heat to a simmer and simmer until it is reduced to about 1 tablespoon (15 ml), about 2 to 4 minutes.

Add the chicken stock, grilled peach purée, white pepper, allspice and salt and whisk well.

Simmer the mixture until bubbles spread evenly across the pan and the mixture can coat the back of a spoon without dripping, about 5 to 7 minutes. Stir in the butter until it's melted. Serve hot over pork chops or as a glaze on grilled pork kebabs.

SLOW ROASTED TOMATO AND CERIGNOLA RELISH

This Tomato and Cerignola Relish is one of our favorites because it's so incredibly versatile. We particularly like the salty-sweet bite of the olives paired with caramelized-tartness of slow roasted tomatoes that makes this hearty enough for a good beefsteak while still being bright enough for fish or grilled chicken. We also love to simply spread this relish on crackers or crostini.

MAKES: about 1 cup (240 ml)   **PREP TIME:** 15 minutes   **COOK TIME:** 1 hour 5 minutes

16 oz (454 g) cherry or teardrop tomatoes, sliced lengthwise

7 cloves garlic, sliced

2 tsp (4 g) minced thyme

¼ tsp sugar

¾ cup (180 ml) olive oil, divided

Zest and juice of 2 lemons

¼ cup (15 g) chopped Italian parsley

¼ cup (45 g) pitted cerignola olives, julienned

Salt and pepper to taste

Preheat the oven to 300°F (149°C).

In a large bowl, toss together the tomatoes, garlic, thyme, sugar and ½ cup (120 ml) of the olive oil.

Arrange the tomatoes flesh side down on a sheet tray or cookie sheet lined with parchment paper and roast slowly for 1 hour or until the tomatoes start to get caramelized and brown and the skin begins to pull away from the flesh.

Remove the tomatoes and allow them to cool, then place them in a large bowl and add the remaining olive oil, lemon zest, lemon juice, parsley, olives and salt and pepper to taste. Toss well. Serve over beefsteak or swordfish steak or grilled chicken.

GOCHUJANG AND SAKE BARBECUE SAUCE

Gochujang is an extremely hot Korean pepper paste made from the gochugaru chili. It is the special ingredient in Korean barbecue, kimchee and many stews. Once a rare ingredient, it's now available as gochujang paste in the international section of most grocery stores. Feel free to reduce the amount of gochujang if you like, as it really is quite spicy.

With the heat from the gochujang, the sweetness of the honey and hoisin sauce and the umami (meatiness) from the fish sauce and soy sauce, this barbecue sauce is ideal for grilled meats like pork and beef. Used more sparingly, it's good on chicken too (dark meat is best). We like to use this sauce on baby back rib racks and it's particularly good for pulled pork.

MAKES: about 1¾ cups (420 ml) **PREP TIME:** 10 minutes **COOK TIME:** 15 minutes

2 tbsp (30 ml) safflower oil

5 scallions, trimmed, white parts only, minced

2 tbsp (43 g) minced garlic

3 tbsp (27 g) freshly grated ginger

⅓ cup (80 ml) tomato paste

¼ cup (60 ml) gochujang paste

¼ cup (60 ml) sake

¼ cup (60 ml) water

¼ cup (60 ml) hoisin sauce

¼ cup (60 ml) honey

1 tbsp (15 ml) fish sauce

1 tbsp (15 ml) soy sauce

Heat a medium saucepan over medium heat and add the safflower oil. Add the scallions, garlic and ginger and sauté for 1 to 2 minutes or until the scallions are softened but the garlic is not too brown.

Stir in the tomato paste and cook, stirring for 1 to 2 minutes.

Add the gochujang paste, sake, water, hoisin, honey, fish sauce and soy sauce and whisk to combine. Reduce the heat to medium-low and simmer the mixture for 8 to 10 minutes, whisking often. Remove from the heat and cool.

Brush the sauce on grilling meats or use afterward as a barbecue sauce.

PINOT NOIR AND CASSAREEP PAN SAUCE

Cassareep is made from the juice of the yuca (cassava), a tropical tuber. The yuca is grated and its liquid is pressed out then boiled with various spices to create a dark, aromatic syrup. When raw, both the yuca and its juice are toxic, but when cooked they are perfectly fine. In fact, yuca is the basis for tapioca.

Cassareep is a specialty of Guyana that has made its way through the Caribbean and is a critical ingredient in the hearty beef stew known as pepperpot. Here we use it to flavor a red wine pan sauce to add a slight bittersweet edge to the plummy red wine, marrying old and new world flavors to the best taste advantage. This pan sauce is excellent for a bone-in steak like a porterhouse or for grilled game meats like venison or elk.

MAKES: ½ cup (120 ml)   **PREP TIME:** 10 minutes   **COOK TIME:** 15 minutes

2 tsp (10 ml) safflower oil

2 tbsp (18 g) minced shallot

¼ tsp minced fresh thyme

½ tsp tomato paste

½ cup (120 ml) pinot noir

1¼ cups (300 ml) Meat Stock (page 14)

1½ tbsp (22 ml) cassareep

¼ tsp salt

⅛ tsp cayenne pepper

1 tbsp (15 g) cold butter

Heat a medium saucepan over medium heat and add the safflower oil. Add the shallot and thyme and sauté until the shallot is softened, about 2 to 3 minutes.

Stir in the tomato paste and cook, stirring for 1 minute.

Pour in the pinot noir and simmer until the liquid is reduced down to 1 tablespoon (15 ml), about 7 to 8 minutes.

Add the beef stock and cassareep and simmer until bubbles form evenly across the surface of the pan and the sauce can evenly coat the back of a spoon without dripping, about 8 to 9 minutes.

Season with salt and cayenne pepper and remove the pan from the heat.

Add the butter and swirl or whisk until melted. Serve with grilled beef or game meats or brushed as a finishing sauce onto braised oxtails.

BURNT SUGAR WITH SCOTCH BONNET STEAK SAUCE

This sauce is a riff on the Caribbean method of stewing meats by first caramelizing sugar to a dark brown then adding seasonings and water. In this thick steak sauce we use both brown sugar and molasses to create layers of flavor.

Scotch bonnet or habañero peppers are commonly used in Caribbean stew sauces and they are incredibly hot—that's why we only call for ¼ of one small pepper in this sauce. Of course you can add more as you like. Whenever you work with extremely hot peppers we suggest using gloves and keeping white vinegar handy—it's extremely effective for removing the pepper oils from counters, knives, cutting boards and hands. Another key seasoning in this sauce is *culantro*, a tropical herb similar in flavor to cilantro but without the soapy aftertaste many people perceive from cilantro. If you can't find it, substitute cilantro instead.

MAKES: 2 cups (480 ml)   **PREP TIME:** 10 minutes   **COOK TIME:** 30 minutes

---

2 tbsp (30 ml) safflower oil

1 small shallot, minced

2 cloves garlic, minced

1 tsp (2 g) fresh thyme, minced

1 tbsp (4 g) chopped culantro or cilantro

2 tsp (10 g) dark brown sugar

¼ small scotch bonnet (habañero) pepper, stemmed, seeded and minced finely

½ cup (120 ml) spiced rum

1 tbsp (15 ml) tomato paste

1 cup (240 ml) tomato purée

1¼ cups (300 ml) Meat Stock (page 14)

2 tbsp (30 ml) molasses

2 tbsp (30 ml) Worcestershire sauce

½ tsp allspice

⅛ tsp ground cloves

½ tsp salt

Heat a medium saucepan over medium heat and add the safflower oil. Add the shallot, garlic and thyme and sauté until the shallot is softened, about 7 to 8 minutes. Stir in the chopped culantro and sauté for 30 seconds more.

Add the sugar and heat, until it becomes caramelized and medium brown in color, about 1 to 2 minutes. Add the scotch bonnet and sauté for about 30 seconds.

Pour in the rum and simmer until the liquid is reduced down to 1 tablespoon (15 ml), about 2 to 4 minutes.

Add the tomato paste and sauté for 1 minute; while whisking add the tomato purée, beef stock, molasses, Worcestershire sauce, allspice, cloves and salt and simmer on medium high for 20 minutes until the mixture is reduced to the texture of marina sauce.

Pour the sauce into a food processor or heavy-duty blender and purée until it is smooth. Return to the pan and simmer for 5 minutes more. Cool and store in an airtight container in the refrigerator. Use as a dipping sauce for steak.

SOUR CHERRY CHILI SAUCE

Sour cherries riff off the jammy qualities of a good quality zinfandel for this sauce that is ideal with a pork roast or thick center cut pork chop. Cinnamon adds additional warmth to the sauce while black pepper offers a touch of heat. Brown sugar sweetens the sauce just a touch. This sauce is very nice on barbecue meats as well.

MAKES: 1 cup (240 ml)   **PREP TIME:** 10 minutes   **COOK TIME:** 40 minutes

2 tsp (10 ml) safflower oil

1 small yellow onion, minced

3 cloves garlic, minced

¾ cup (180 ml) zinfandel

1 cinnamon stick

1 bay leaf

1 cup (240 ml) tart cherry juice

½ tsp ground chipotle pepper

1 tbsp (5 g) dark brown sugar

¼ tsp salt or to taste

Heat the safflower oil in a medium saucepan over medium heat and add the onion. Sauté the onion until softened, about 5 to 6 minutes. Add the garlic and sauté for 1 to 2 minutes more.

Pour in the zinfandel, cinnamon stick and bay leaf and reduce heat to a simmer. Reduce the wine by half, about 8 to 9 minutes.

Pour in the tart cherry juice and mix well.

Stir in the chipotle pepper, and dark brown sugar. Simmer for 15 to 20 minutes or until the mixture is reduced by about half. Stir in the salt and adjust to taste. Remove the bay leaf and cinnamon stick before serving. Store in a tightly sealed jar in the refrigerator for up to 1 week or serve warm over filet mignon.

ROOT BEER GLAZE

Some folks will raise their eyebrows at the use of root beer soda for this glaze while others will recognize it as similar to the old Southern technique of incorporating cola into pot roast. We love the cinnamon and anise flavors of root beer when paired with pork, and we use this glaze when cooking ham and pork tenderloin, glazing them as they cook. In the summer, we serve this sauce as an accompaniment to grilled pork chops. It's really important to use a great root beer like Barq's brand for this glaze.

MAKES: 1½ cups (360 ml)   **PREP TIME:** 5 minutes   **COOK TIME:** 30 to 35 minutes

3 cups (720 ml) root beer

¾ cup (165 g) packed brown sugar

½ cup (120 ml) ketchup

¼ cup (60 ml) white wine vinegar

3 tbsp (45 ml) steak sauce

1 tbsp (15 ml) Dijon mustard

1 tsp (5 ml) Sriracha sauce

¼ tsp ground cloves

Combine all the ingredients in a large saucepan over medium-high heat. Bring the mixture to a boil then reduce to a simmer and cook until the liquid is reduced by half, about 30 minutes. Brush onto a baked ham while it is cooking or as a glaze for pork chops.

CORIANDER AND GINGER GLAZE

Glaze or, in French, glacé, is a simple technique that requires time as the main ingredient. The goal is to boil unsalted beef stock until it is a thick, syrupy and shiny sauce. We recommend making your own stock for glazes, but if you use store bought, be sure it is sodium-free or the final product will be extremely salty as a result of the reduction process. Glazes like this one have any number of uses, but this one has a snap of spicy ginger along with the slightly astringent quality of coriander seeds that is extremely nice with tender cuts of beef. Use it sparingly as the flavor is intense.

MAKES: ½ cup (120 ml)   **PREP TIME:** 10 minutes   **COOK TIME:** about 1 hour

1-inch (25-mm) piece peeled ginger

1 tsp (2 g) whole coriander, slightly crushed

3 cups (720 ml) Meat Stock (page 14)

¼ tsp salt

¼ tsp black pepper

In a medium saucepan, combine the ginger, coriander and meat stock and bring to a simmer.

Simmer this mixture until it is reduced by half, about 45 to 50 minutes. Strain the stock through a fine mesh sieve lined with a cheesecloth into a smaller pot.

Continue to simmer the strained stock until it is reduced about three-quarters, or until it is thick and syrupy, about 20 minutes. You should have roughly ½ cup (120 ml) of glaze. Whisk in the salt and pepper. Use immediately with sliced pork or beef tenderloin or refrigerate in a well sealed container for up to 1 week.

CUBAN MOJO

Mojo is a popular Cuban sauce that is most often used as a marinade for pork or a condiment with starchy tubers like cassava (yuca). The recipe for mojo can vary from region to town to family but the foundational components are garlic, oregano and a fat, which historically was lard but nowadays is olive oil, and Seville orange juice. Seville oranges, also called bitter oranges, offer an extremely tart, acidic juice that is particularly good accompanying fatty meat or as a tenderizing marinade and braising liquid for tougher meat, like goat.

We like to add a little bit of habañero pepper to our mojo for a sauce that is a spicy, tart and herbaceous.

MAKES: about 3 cups (720 ml)   **PREP TIME:** 10 minutes   **COOK TIME:** 5 minutes

2 shallots, minced

10 cloves garlic minced

½ cup (30 g) chopped fresh oregano

½ cup (30 g) chopped fresh culantro or cilantro

¼ habañero pepper, stemmed and seeded

½ tsp ground coriander

½ tsp ground cumin

2 tsp (12 g) salt

1 cup (240 ml) olive oil, divided

1½ cups (360 ml) Seville orange juice

Place the shallots, garlic, oregano, culantro, habañero pepper, coriander, cumin and salt in a food processor, add 1 tablespoon (15 ml) of the olive oil and process to create a thick, smooth paste. Add more oil if necessary to create the paste.

Add the Seville orange juice and continue to process.

Slowly drizzle in the remaining olive oil while processing until you get a thick, frothy sauce. Serve as a condiment or use as a marinade for meat. Store in an airtight jar in the refrigerator for up to 1 week. Use for braising goat, stewing beef or brushed on a barbecued pork shoulder.

BUCCANEER CHIMICHURRI

This sauce is based on a Caribbean multi-herb flavoring paste called Green Seasoning. Originally it was a mixture used to season and flavor game meats before they were smoked for preservation in a process said to be created by the Buccaneers—the original pirates of the Caribbean.

We like to process the paste into a smooth sauce, with the addition of a good quality olive oil and lime juice to replace the white vinegar that is traditionally used. Because this sauce is an explosion of green herb flavor, it can be used either as a marinade, a brushing sauce for barbecue meats or even like a chimichurri on top of a beef or lamb burger or grilled steak.

MAKES: 2 cups (480 ml)   **PREP TIME:** 10 minutes   **COOK TIME:** 5 minutes

2 bunches flat leaf parsley, leaves only

2 bunches culantro or cilantro, leaves only

1 bunch scallions, trimmed

1 bunch fresh oregano, leaves only

1 bunch fresh thyme, leaves only

3 shallots

10 cloves garlic

½ habañero pepper, stemmed and seeded

1 tbsp (18 g) salt

½ cup (120 ml) freshly squeezed lime juice or more as needed

1 cup (240 ml) olive oil

Place the parsley, culantro, scallions, oregano and thyme in a food processor and process to a rough paste.

Add the shallots, garlic, habañero pepper and salt and continue to process until the paste becomes smoother, about 1 minute.

Pour in the lime juice slowly, while processing, until you achieve a smooth paste.

Add the oil in a thin stream while processing until the sauce is thick and well incorporated. Store in an airtight jar in the refrigerator for up to 1 week. Serve as a topping on beef or lamb burgers or just before serving a grilled steak like London broil.

THE ULTIMATE ROAST BEEF GRAVY

Like our Go-To Gravy (page 53) this sauce uses roux as the beginnings of a smooth, almost nutty flavored gravy. Beef broth is the basis for a richer gravy than the one we use for poultry, and rosemary is a perfect herb accompaniment to red meat, but you'll note we use it sparingly as it can be overpowering. Use pan drippings for both grease and stock if you have them for the best flavored gravy.

MAKES: 1 cup (240 ml)   **PREP TIME:** 5 minutes   **COOK TIME:** 10 minutes

3 tbsp (45 g) butter or pan grease from roast beef

2 tbsp (17 g) flour

1½ cups (360 ml) Meat Stock (page 14)

¼ tsp minced rosemary

¼ tsp minced thyme leaves

¼ tsp celery salt

¼ tsp white pepper

Melt the butter or heat the pan grease in a medium saucepan over medium heat.

Add the flour and whisk well until it is completely incorporated into the butter or fat. Continue to cook, whisking, until the flour is a deep golden brown, about 4 to 5 minutes.

Add the beef stock and whisk well until the mixture is completely combined.

Reduce the heat to a simmer and add the rosemary, thyme leaves, celery salt and white pepper. Simmer 2 to 4 minutes more or until the mixture is thick enough to coat the back of a spoon. Taste to adjust the salt. Serve hot with roast beef.

SAUCES FOR
Vegetables & Pasta

Vegetables and sauces have long had an uneasy relationship. Produce purists tout the fresh flavor of farm goods without the need for sauces to drown their true essence. On the other hand, many a parent knows the benefit of a sauce or dip to make vegetables palatable to young eaters.

We advocate an approach that is something in the middle—a good sauce can enhance a vegetable's natural flavor and raise it to new heights, making it all the more appealing. In some cases, the sauces we suggest are made from other vegetables in another form like the Grilled Japanese Eggplant and Roasted Tomato Sauce (page 137), which adds a whole layer of texture as well as taste to your veggies.

As with any sauce, we suggest a light hand when using on vegetables in order to create a true partnership of ingredients rather than using it to overpower the target food's real flavor.

PIMENTO CHEESE WITH TEQUILA MORNAY

Pimento cheese is a mixture of sharp cheddar cheese, pimentos and seasonings that is incredibly popular as a spread or dip in the South. The tangy and spicy flavors make it a delicious sauce for a variety of uses from chicken to vegetables and pasta—particularly as a new twist on macaroni and cheese. We make ours using the classic technique for Mornay—Béchamel sauce enriched with cheese—then add a zing with a splash of tequila. The sauce may be made ahead and refrigerated. Before using, reheat the sauce in a medium saucepan over low heat with ¼ cup (60 ml) of milk.

MAKES: about 2 cups (480 ml)　　**PREP TIME:** 5 minutes　　**COOK TIME:** 6 minutes

3 tbsp (45 g) butter

3 tbsp (25 g) flour

2 tbsp (24 g) drained and minced jarred pimentos

1 cup (240 ml) milk

1 cup (113 g) shredded sharp cheddar cheese

½ tsp salt

¼ tsp cayenne pepper

1 tbsp (15 ml) tequila

Melt the butter in a medium saucepan over medium heat and add the flour. Whisk well and continue whisking while the mixture cooks and begins to lightly brown, about 2 minutes.

Add the pimentos and whisk well. Cook for 1 minute.

Pour in the milk and continue to whisk and simmer the mixture until it thickens, about 2 to 3 minutes.

Add the shredded cheese and whisk well to melt. Stir in the salt and cayenne pepper and cook for 1 minute. Remove from the heat and stir in the tequila. Use immediately over steamed or sautéed vegetables, as a dip, as the basis for macaroni and cheese or refrigerate for up to 3 days.

BROCCOLI PESTO

A different take on traditional pesto, this version uses almonds in place of pine nuts and adds broccoli florets for an intensely green sneaky sauce that lets you add more vegetables into your diet under the cover of aromatic basil, tangy capers, garlic and salty parmesan. This sauce is great on chicken, pasta or grilled vegetables, and we've even used it as a tasty dip.

MAKES: 2 cups (480 ml) **PREP TIME:** 10 minutes **COOK TIME:** 10 minutes

½ lb (227 g) broccoli florets

2 cloves garlic, peeled and lightly smashed

½ cup (72 g) toasted almonds

2 tbsp (17 g) capers

1 cup (60 g) tightly packed basil leaves

⅓ to ½ cup (80 to 120 ml) extra virgin olive oil

Salt and pepper, to taste

⅓ cup (60 g) freshly grated Parmesan cheese

Steam the broccoli for 6 minutes, until very tender but still bright. Remove from the heat, rinse with cold water and drain well.

Place the broccoli in the food processor with the garlic and almonds and process to a rough paste. Scrape down the sides of the bowl and add the capers and the basil and process to a smooth paste.

Continue to process while drizzling in the olive oil and purée until smooth. Add salt and pepper to taste, the grated cheese and pulse a few more times to blend completely. Use with hot or cold cooked pasta or over grilled vegetables.

CARAMELIZED GARLIC AND SHALLOT WHITE WINE SAUCE

This creamy, slightly pungent sauce is excellent over virtually any vegetable or pasta. It can be enhanced by adding a sprinkle of Parmesan or even gruyere cheese after serving. Minced mushrooms sautéed with the aromatics is another lovely addition too. However, the sauce is absolutely excellent served as is. We like to use a good quality chardonnay wine for this sauce because of the buttery characteristics of that oak-aged quaff.

MAKES: 1 cup (240 ml)　　**PREP TIME:** 10 minutes　　**COOK TIME:** 10 to 12 minutes

1 tbsp (15 g) butter

2 shallots, minced

5 cloves garlic, sliced thinly

1 tsp (2 g) fresh minced thyme leaves

½ cup (120 ml) chardonnay

1½ cups (360 ml) heavy cream

½ tsp salt or to taste

⅛ tsp nutmeg

Freshly ground black pepper to taste

2 tbsp (8 g) freshly chopped parsley

Melt the butter in a medium saucepan over medium heat and add the shallots and garlic. Reduce the heat to medium-low and gently sauté until the garlic begins to become deep golden brown, about 2 to 3 minutes.

Stir in the thyme leaves and sauté for 15 to 30 seconds then add the chardonnay and simmer until reduced to about 1 tablespoon (15 ml), about 5 to 6 minutes.

Add the cream, salt, nutmeg and pepper. Mix well and simmer this mixture until it reduces by one third and is thick enough to coat the back of a spoon, about 8 to 10 minutes.

Stir in the freshly chopped parsley and serve hot over pasta or cooked vegetables like green beans or asparagus.

GORGONZOLA WHITE WINE SAUCE

If you are a blue cheese lover, this is the sauce for you. We like to use sweet Gorgonzola cheese that is brightened by a chardonnay wine reduction. Good for any pasta with ridges and curves to which this sauce can cling, we find it's also tasty on roasted potatoes.

MAKES: 2 cups (480 ml)   **PREP TIME:** 5 minutes   **COOK TIME:** 20 to 25 minutes

1 tbsp (15 g) butter

2 tbsp (30 g) minced shallot

½ cup (120 ml) chardonnay

2 sprigs fresh thyme

1¾ cups (420 ml) heavy cream

4 oz (112 g) sweet Gorgonzola

½ tsp salt

½ tsp white pepper

¼ cup (15 g) freshly chopped parsley

Melt the butter in a medium saucepan over medium heat and add the shallot. Sauté until the shallot is softened, about 2 to 3 minutes.

Add the chardonnay and the thyme sprigs and simmer until the wine is reduced to 1 to 2 tablespoons (15 to 30 ml), about 7 to 9 minutes.

Stir in the heavy cream and simmer until the cream is thickened and reduced to just over a cup (240 ml). Add the cheese and mix well to melt.

Season with the salt and pepper, adding more to taste as desired and stir in the fresh parsley. Serve hot over roasted potatoes or green beans.

CURRY BUTTER SAUCE

This incredibly easy sauce is great on all kinds of vegetables from roasted potatoes and other root vegetables to baked squash, lightly sautéed or steamed zucchini, green beans, red peppers and more. It is particularly excellent on roasted cauliflower—simply drizzle the sauce on the cauliflower before baking and reserve some for serving. It is also delicious on cooked rice or couscous.

Since the sauce has only three ingredients it's important to make the most of each one, so choose a good quality, aromatic Madras curry powder. You'll note that we are calling for ghee or clarified butter for this sauce. Clarified butter offers a nutty taste and a clear sauce that isn't clouded by milk solids. You can find it in gourmet stores or Indian markets.

MAKES: ½ cup (120 ml)   **PREP TIME:** 5 minutes   **COOK TIME:** 7 minutes

4 oz (110 g) ghee or clarified butter

4 cloves garlic, minced

1 tbsp (9 g) Madras curry powder

Melt the ghee in a small sauté pan over medium heat and add the garlic. Cook until the garlic begins to lightly brown, about 5 to 6 minutes.

Whisk in the curry powder and cook for 1 minute more, or until the curry releases its aromas. Drizzle over vegetables—it is particularly good on roasted cauliflower or rice.

SAGE BROWN BUTTER SAUCE

Another incredibly easy sauce that is good with all manner of vegetables and pasta. Nutty from the browned butter with the comforting flavor of herby sage, this sauce packs a lot of flavor while still being light. We particularly like to serve this with pan-fried gnocchi, but it is excellent with couscous, quinoa and almost any pasta.

MAKES: ½ cup (120 ml)　　**PREP TIME:** 5 minutes　　**COOK TIME:** 12 minutes

12 tbsp (180 g) good quality butter

3 sage leaves

Melt the butter in a small saucepan over medium-low heat. Raise the heat enough to allow the butter to lightly simmer and allow to cook until the butter foams.

When the foam dies down, continue to simmer the butter until it browns and the milk solids darken and fall to the bottom of the pan—about 8 to 10 minutes.

Pour the browned butter through a fine mesh sieve into another saucepan over medium heat and add the sage leaves. Fry until the sage leaves crisp and curl, less than 1 minute. Serve over pasta or vegetables. It is a lovely sauce to go with pumpkin ravioli.

SPICY RED PEPPER AIOLI

Aioli is essentially a mayonnaise to which garlic paste has been added. It's very easy to make but is sure to impress your guests. We use this spicy aioli as a drizzle on fish stew and steamed clams. It adds a delicious layer of heat and creaminess to the dish. If you want the spice to be milder, substitute mild paprika for the hot and keep the cayenne pepper.

MAKES: 1 cup (240 ml)   **PREP TIME:** 10 minutes   **COOK TIME:** None

2 egg yolks

½ tsp Dijon mustard

2 tsp (10 ml) lemon juice

¼ cup (60 ml) safflower oil

¼ cup (60 ml) olive oil

2 cloves garlic, crushed to a paste

4 tsp (9 g) hot paprika

¼ tsp cayenne

Combine all the ingredients in a blender and process on high until the mixture comes together into a thick sauce, slightly looser than mayonnaise. Use as a dip for crudite, as a side for grilled vegetables or use as a sandwich or burger condiment.

COCONUT NECTAR, PINEAPPLE AND THYME GLAZE

This is a good fruity glaze for roasted hearty fall and winter vegetables such as carrots, parsnips, hard squashes and sweet potatoes. It also serves double duty as a nice finish sauce on roasted chicken slices. Try to get pineapple juice in a carton versus a can since the can often adds a metallic taste to the finished sauce. Coconut nectar is sometimes called coconut molasses and is available in most gourmet stores or the natural aisle of conventional supermarkets.

MAKES: 1 cup (240 ml)   **PREP TIME:** 5 minutes   **COOK TIME:** 15 minutes

1 tsp (5 g) coconut oil

1 small shallot, minced

1 tbsp (4 g) freshly minced thyme leaves

1 cup (240 ml) coconut nectar

¾ cup (180 ml) fresh pineapple juice

¼ tsp salt

Freshly ground black pepper to taste

Heat the coconut oil in a medium saucepan over medium heat and add the shallot. Sauté until the shallot softens, about 2 to 3 minutes.

Add the thyme leaves and sauté 1 minute more.

Stir in the coconut nectar and pineapple juice and whisk well. Season with salt and pepper. Simmer until the mixture is reduced by about two-thirds, or until it is the consistency of thick maple syrup, about 10 to 12 minutes. It will also thicken as it cools. Serve with roasted vegetables like cubed kabocha squash.

GRILLED JAPANESE EGGPLANT AND ROASTED TOMATO SAUCE

We like to grill the eggplant for this sauce because it lends a smoky, almost meaty quality to the sauce. This is an excellent do-ahead sauce because you can cook the eggplant earlier in the day or the day before and complete the sauce after the tomatoes come out of the oven. We use Japanese eggplant for this sauce because it is thin-skinned and not as bitter as Italian varieties. This sauce is just as good at room temperature as it is hot. Use this sauce as a different twist on traditional tomato-based pasta sauces.

MAKES: about 3 cups (720 ml)   **PREP TIME:** 10 minutes   **COOK TIME:** 1 hour

1 lb (454 g) Japanese eggplant, trimmed and cut into ½-inch (12 mm) thick slices

⅓ cup (80 ml) extra virgin olive oil, divided

2 cups (300 g) cherry tomatoes, halved

3 cloves garlic, thinly sliced

2 sprigs of thyme, chopped

1 cup (240 ml) Vegetable Stock (page 12)

6 leaves basil, cut finely

½ tsp salt

¼ tsp freshly ground black pepper

Preheat the oven to 400°F (204°C).

Lightly brush the eggplant slices with some of the olive oil and sear on a hot grill, about 2 to 3 minutes per side. Place the eggplant on a cookie sheet to cool. When they are cool enough to handle, roughly chop the eggplant and set aside in a large bowl.

In another bowl, toss together the cherry tomatoes, garlic, remaining olive oil and thyme. Place the tomatoes flat side down on a non-stick sheet pan. Cook in the oven for about 30 to 40 minutes. Remove and cool.

Scrape the grilled Japanese eggplant and tomatoes into the bowl of a food processer and add the vegetable stock, basil, salt and pepper. Process to a rough paste.

Scrape this mixture into a medium saucepan and place over medium heat. Simmer for 2 to 3 minutes so the flavors combine and set aside to cool completely. Adjust salt and pepper to taste. Serve over heartier pasta such as penne or fusilli or over grilled asparagus.

FIDDLEHEAD FERN AND GARLIC PESTO

Fiddlehead ferns are a favorite spring ingredient. They are the furled fronds of a young fern. They have a short season, and their flavor has been compared to other green vegetables including artichokes, asparagus and green beans. When choosing them, look for fiddleheads that are small, firm and tightly furled. You should store them in the refrigerator wrapped tightly in plastic. They won't spoil quickly, but they will lose flavor and firmness after a couple of days. The extra bite from the walnuts and umami flavor from the anchovy fillet makes this a lovely sauce for grilled vegetables, pasta and roasted potatoes.

MAKES: 1½ cups (360 ml) **PREP TIME:** 15 minutes **COOK TIME:** 5 to 7 minutes

¾ cup (100 g) fiddleheads

2 cups (120 g) fresh basil leaves, packed

⅓ cup (35 g) walnuts, toasted and chopped

2 cloves garlic, smashed

1 anchovy filet, chopped

½ to ¾ cup (120 to 180 ml) extra virgin olive oil

¼ cup (25 g) grated pecorino cheese

Cook the fiddleheads in a steamer basket set over a saucepan of boiling water. Steam for 5 to 7 minutes. Remove, rinse with cold water and drain completely.

Place the fiddleheads in a food processor along with the basil, walnut, garlic and anchovy and process into a coarse paste.

While processing, add the oil in a thin stream, pausing to scrape down the sides of the bowl with a rubber spatula as needed.

Scrape the mixture into a bowl and stir in the cheese. Use immediately over roasted baby potatoes, pasta or vegetables. Store, refrigerated, in a tightly sealed container up to 5 days, or portion into small containers and freeze for up to 2 months.

ROASTED PURPLE CARROT AND GINGER SAUCE

Japanese ginger and carrot salad dressing is one of our favorites. We love the combination of sweetness from the carrot and fresh tang of ginger and decided to create a sauce for cooked vegetables that made use of the same flavors.

Here we roast purple heirloom carrots with a little brown sugar before puréeing with ginger and other ingredients for a sauce that works well with steamed or roasted green beans, cauliflower or Brussels sprouts. If you can't find purple carrots, regular orange ones work just as well. For a milder carrot flavor try parsnips.

MAKES: 1 cup (240 ml)   **PREP TIME:** 15 minutes   **COOK TIME:** 1 hour 15 minutes

3 large purple carrots, peeled, trimmed and cut into 1-inch (25-mm) pieces

3 tbsp (45 ml) sesame oil, divided

Salt and pepper to taste

2 tbsp (8 g) sugar, divided

2 tbsp (18 g) grated fresh ginger

1 shallot

1 tbsp (15 ml) freshly squeezed lemon juice

⅓ cup (80 ml) rice wine vinegar or more as needed

1 tbsp (15 ml) soy sauce

Preheat the oven to 400°F (204°C).

Arrange the carrot slices in a single layer on a cookie sheet or baking dish and drizzle with 1 tablespoon (15 ml) of the sesame oil. Season with salt and pepper and 1 tablespoon (4 g) of sugar. Mix well and roast for 45 minutes to 1 hour or until the carrots are fork tender.

When the carrots are cooked, scrape them into the bowl of a food processor along with the remaining sugar, sesame oil, ginger, shallot, lemon juice, rice wine vinegar and soy sauce. Process into a smooth, loose paste, adding rice wine vinegar as needed to achieve this consistency.

Pour the mixture into a medium saucepan over medium heat and bring to a simmer. Simmer 5 to 10 minutes for the flavors to combine. Serve over vegetables or even as a salad dressing. Sauce may be stored, refrigerated, in a well-sealed container for up to 1 week.

GOLDEN BEET SAUCE

This slightly sweet, musky, glossy, yellow-orange sauce is beautiful on a white plate with roasted vegetables set on top or some browned gnocchi. It pairs well with root vegetables like parsnip, turnip and Jerusalem artichokes. Like its red beet counterpart, it's also tasty with potato turnovers, latkes or fritters. We've even served this sauce with Aloo pie, the spicy potato stuffed pastry popular in Trinidad.

MAKES: about 1 cup (240 ml)   **PREP TIME:** 10 minutes   **COOK TIME:** 1 hour 30 minutes

1 medium yellow beet, trimmed

2 tsp (10 ml) olive oil

Salt and pepper

2 cups (480 ml) water plus 1 tbsp (15 ml), divided

2 tsp (10 ml) safflower oil

1 medium carrot, trimmed, peeled and minced

1 rib celery, trimmed, peeled and minced

1 shallot, minced

½ tsp thyme leaves

1 tbsp (8 g) cornstarch

Preheat the oven to 400°F (204°C).

Scrub the beet well and pat dry then place it on a square of tin foil that is large enough to wrap it completely. Drizzle the beet with the olive oil and season well with salt and pepper then wrap it in the foil. Place the wrapped beet on a baking dish and bake until it is tender, about 45 minutes. Remove and peel when the beet is cool enough to handle.

Place the roasted beet in a medium saucepan with 2 cups (480 ml) of water and bring to a simmer. Simmer the beet about 15 to 20 minutes. Remove the beet from the water, reserve the water and allow the beet to cool completely. Grate the beet finely and set aside.

Heat a medium sauté pan over medium heat and add the safflower oil. Add the carrot and celery and sauté until they begin to soften, about 2 minutes. Add the shallot and thyme leaves and cook for 2 minutes more. Stir in the shredded beet and mix well, then sauté for 1 to 2 minutes.

Pour in the beet broth and simmer for 10 to 12 minutes more. Pour the mixture through a fine mesh sieve into a smaller saucepan, pressing on the solids to remove all liquid. Place the saucepan with the cooking liquid over a medium low heat and bring to a simmer.

Dissolve the cornstarch in 1 tablespoon (15 ml) of water so that the mixture resembles heavy cream. Pour the cornstarch into the beet cooking liquid and whisk well. Allow to simmer for 1 minute or until the mixture is thick enough to coat the back of a spoon. Serve with potato turnovers, latke or gnocchi.

SAUCES FOR
Dessert

As if dessert wasn't delightful enough, dessert sauces are the proverbial (and literal!) icing on the cake. Unlike frosting, which can be heavy, sauces are a lovely complement to a variety of desserts from chocolate based to fruit based, ice cream, bread puddings and more. Sometimes sauces are as integral to a plate of dessert as the preparation itself, adding a layer of bright flavor that might not be possible in the main dish.

Because most of our dessert sauces don't contain egg and any milk product is cooked, you'll find that they store nicely—in most cases for up to a week. This is a great boon if you have a sweet tooth and want to keep a little something extra around to enliven store-bought ice cream, pound cake or pie.

HIBISCUS SYRUP

We absolutely love the syrup made from dried roselle hibiscus flowers. Hibiscus syrup is common in Central America and the Caribbean, where it is the basis of a traditional drink called *sorrel*. Our hibiscus syrup is the perfect mix of sweet and tart. We make a batch of this and keep in the refrigerator to use in place of syrup over pancakes. It's also wonderful with poppy seed cake and as an accompaniment to iced tea.

MAKES: 2 cups (480 ml)　　**PREP TIME:** 5 minutes　　**COOK TIME:** 45 minutes

2 cups (480 ml) water

1 cup (200 g) granulated sugar

¾ cup (8 g) dried hibiscus flowers

½ tsp freshly squeezed lemon juice

½ vanilla bean

Combine the water, sugar and hibiscus flowers in a large saucepan. Bring to a boil, stirring occasionally and continue to simmer until a thick syrup forms, about 12 to 15 minutes.

Remove from the heat and stir in the lemon juice. Split the vanilla bean lengthwise and scrape out the seeds. Add both the seeds and the bean to the hibiscus mixture.

Let the mixture steep for 30 minutes then strain through a fine sieve. Strain again through a cheesecloth to remove fine powdered hibiscus debris.

Let the syrup stand at room temperature until cool, about 1 hour, then transfer to an airtight jar or bottle and refrigerate for up to 3 weeks. Serve with pancakes, waffles, cake or light mousses.

EXTRA DARK MEXICAN CHOCOLATE SAUCE

Who doesn't love a good chocolate sauce? Velvety smooth and deliciously decadent, chocolate sauce can be drizzled on anything from ice cream to brownies to cheesecake, or it can flavor a milk shake and more. In our version, we combine both dark chocolate and black (ultra-Dutched) cocoa powder, a much more intense version that is available in baking supply and gourmet spice stores.

MAKES: about 2½ cups (600 ml)　　**PREP TIME:** 10 minutes　　**COOK TIME:** 15 minutes

8 oz (224 g) 70% bittersweet chocolate, chopped

1 cup (240 ml) heavy cream

½ cup (120 ml) light corn syrup

½ tbsp (3 g) black chocolate powder

¼ tsp ground chipotle pepper

⅛ tsp salt

½ tsp ground cinnamon

Pinch of ground cloves

1 tbsp (15 g) butter

Place the chocolate pieces in a metal bowl.

Combine the heavy cream, corn syrup, chocolate powder, chipotle pepper, salt and cinnamon in a medium saucepan over medium heat and whisk well to combine. Bring the mixture to just under a simmer, about 3 to 5 minutes.

Pour the cream mixture over the chocolate and let sit for 3 to 4 minutes or until the chocolate melts. Add the butter and whisk very well to achieve a smooth sauce. Serve over ice cream or vanilla cake like a fudge sauce. Store refrigerated in a tightly sealed container for up to 2 weeks. Reheat sauce in a double boiler or 10 seconds at a time in the microwave, mixing often.

SWEET ALMOND AND CARDAMOM CREAM SAUCE

This sauce is an essentially crème anglaise enriched with almond butter and almond extract. Crème anglaise is the classic French vanilla sweet-cream sauce that is the base for vanilla ice cream and crème brûlée.

You must use whole milk rather than lower fat varieties or the sauce won't set. Almond butter is available in most supermarkets as an alternative to peanut butter. Make sure you get an extra smooth variety. Vanilla bean really puts this sauce into the realm of the spectacular. Cardamom and almond are a pairing common in the Middle East, and a flavor that was very popular in Europe during the Medieval period. The cardamom adds an almost minty aroma and flavor to the sauce that makes it an ideal pairing with fruit-based desserts like an apple or pear strudel.

MAKES: 1½ cups (360 ml)   **PREP TIME:** 15 minutes   **COOK TIME:** 30 to 40 minutes

½ cup (120 ml) milk

½ cup (120 ml) heavy cream

1 vanilla bean

¼ tsp cardamom

2 tsp (10 g) almond butter

1 tsp (5 ml) almond extract

3 egg yolks

3 tbsp (38 g) sugar

Combine the milk and heavy cream in a medium saucepan. Using a sharp paring knife, score the vanilla bean lengthwise and scrape out the seeds. Add the seeds and the whole bean to the pot with the milk and cream and set over medium heat.

Bring the milk mixture to just under a simmer, about 3 to 4 minutes. Whisk in the cardamom, almond butter and almond extract. Whisk very well to combine and ensure the almond butter is melted. Bring the milk to a simmer once again.

Combine the egg yolks and sugar in a medium bowl and whisk very well to combine. Remove the vanilla bean from the milk mixture then slowly add the hot milk mixture to the egg yolks in a thin stream, while whisking vigorously.

When all the milk has been added to the yolks, pour the whole mixture through a fine mesh sieve back in to the saucepan over medium-low heat. Cook the crème anglaise until it thickens, while whisking, about 5 to 6 minutes. Do not allow the mixture to boil. When the crème coats the back of a spoon without dripping it is ready.

Chill the crème in a bowl with plastic wrap placed right against the surface of the crème. Serve chilled with pear or apple strudel.

RUM AND ORANGE GLAZE

This wonderfully simple dessert sauce has a lovely orange flavor and hue that is made even more tropical with the spicy sweetness of rum, star anise cinnamon. It is quite nice for dressing up simple desserts like pound cake or angel food cake. The rum is a key flavor component so use the best quality rum that you can find. We like to use a good quality orange marmalade with bits of visible orange zest because it makes for a nice presentation within the finished sauce.

MAKES: ⅔ cup (160 ml)   **PREP TIME:** 5 minutes   **COOK TIME:** 30 minutes

⅓ cup (80 ml) orange marmalade

⅓ cup (80 ml) water

⅓ cup (80 ml) dark rum

1 cinnamon stick

1 star anise pod

Combine the marmalade, water and rum in a small saucepan and whisk very well to combine.

Add the cinnamon stick and star anise pod and heat over medium heat. Bring the mixture to a boil then lower the heat to a simmer. Simmer the sauce until it is reduced to a syrup, about 18 to 20 minutes. Allow it to cool completely, then remove the cinnamon stick and star anise. Store in an airtight jar. Serve with pound cake or angel food cake.

PASSION FRUIT AND COGNAC SYRUP

Passion fruit is brightly colored yellow, sweet-tart tropical fruit that is quite nice with vanilla custard, panna cotta or a lemon mousse. The fruit is pulpy and full of seeds, however, so we like to use a passion fruit purée concentrate, like the one available at Perfect Purée, for this preparation, which is more syrup than sauce. The cognac is just a flavoring agent so mix it in after the syrup is prepared and cooled.

MAKES: 1½ cups (360 ml)　　**PREP TIME:** 5 minutes　　**COOK TIME:** 30 minutes

1 cup (240 ml) water

2 cups (400 g) sugar

¼ cup (60 ml) passion fruit purée

1 tbsp (15 ml) cognac

Combine the water and sugar in a small saucepan and bring to a simmer. Whisk well to combine and dissolve the sugar.

Continue to simmer until the mixture is reduced to a thick syrup, about 26 to 28 minutes.

Stir in the passion fruit purée and cognac and remove from the heat. Chill and store in a sealed container for up to 5 days. Serve with vanilla custard, crème brûlée or coconut panna cotta.

SWEET PICKLED GINGER

You'll recognize pickled ginger if you've ever eaten in a sushi restaurant. It is the pale pink condiment that you see on the side of your plate. With its mix of aromatic heat and sweetness, our version is excellent not just as a side dish to sushi but as a garnishment to desserts, particularly those that have more of an Eastern twist. Younger ginger rhizomes are less woody and more tender, plus only young ginger will have a pink tinge when pickled, so we recommend you try to get those for this recipe.

MAKES: about 2 cups (480 ml) **PREP TIME:** 10 minutes **COOK TIME:** 10 minutes

14 oz (392 g) ginger, preferably young

2 quarts (2 L) plus 3 tbsp (45 ml) water, divided

9 tbsp (135 ml) rice vinegar

2¾ tsp (13 g) kosher salt, divided

5 to 6 tbsp (63 to 75 g) sugar, or to taste

Peel the ginger and cut it lengthwise into paper-thin slices 1 to 1½ inches (25 to 38 mm) long.

In a small saucepan, combine 3 tablespoons (45 ml) of water, the rice vinegar, 2½ teaspoons (15 g) of salt and the sugar, and bring the mixture to a boil over medium heat. Cook the mixture, stirring, until the sugar and salt are dissolved. Turn off the heat, and transfer the liquid to a clean quart container with a tight-fitting lid.

In a medium pot, bring about 2 quarts (2 L) of water to a boil over high heat. Add the ginger slices all at once, and blanch them for 20 seconds if you're using young ginger, or 30 to 40 seconds if the ginger is mature. Drain the ginger in a large, flat-bottomed colander, spreading the slices so that they dry quickly. Sprinkle the remaining ¼ teaspoon salt over the ginger slices, and toss gently.

While the ginger slices are still hot, transfer them to the ready container of pickling liquid. When the ginger slices contact the vinegar, they will turn a pretty, faint pink color. Refrigerate the ginger for two days, covered, before using. Use on top of ice cream, to garnish panacotta or even as a side condiment to fish.

GUAVA AND GINGER GLAZE

Guava and ginger combine in this glaze for a bright tropical flavor profile that is wonderful for homemade donuts, sweet fritters like beignet or even scones. It is particularly good on banana cake.

MAKES: 1 cup (240 ml) **PREP TIME:** 5 minutes **COOK TIME:** 10 minutes

1½ tbsp (22 ml) water

1¼ tsp (6 ml) freshly squeezed lemon juice

1 tsp (3 g) powdered ginger

¼ cup (60 ml) guava jelly

2 cups (240 g) powdered sugar

Combine all the ingredients in a small sauce pan and whisk well. Simmer for 7 to 8 minutes. Remove from heat and cool. Use as a glaze on your favorite donut, beignet or scone.

CANDIED RHUBARB SAUCE

This is a saucy version of strawberry rhubarb pie filling, enlivened with ginger, a spice we love for its warmth and brightness. In this preparation, we are using crystallized rather than fresh ginger, which adds an almost jammy quality to this sauce, which is more like a compote. Use this over pancakes, waffles, pound cake or angel food cake. It's also excellent drizzled over the top of strawberry shortcakes as a garnish.

MAKES: 3 cups (720 ml)   **PREP TIME:** 10 minutes   **COOK TIME:** 15 minutes

2 lbs (910 g) strawberries, halved if large, divided

1 lb (454 g) rhubarb, trimmed and cut into ¾-inch (2-cm) pieces

½ cup (100 g) sugar

3 tbsp (20 g) minced crystallized ginger

1 tbsp (15 ml) fresh lime juice

¾ tsp grated lime peel

¼ cup (60 ml) water

Place 1½ pounds (680 g) of strawberries and all the rhubarb in a medium pot. Mix in the sugar, ginger, lime juice and peel and ¼ cup (60 ml) of water.

Cover the pot and cook over high heat until the sugar dissolves, stirring often. Boil the mixture for 4 minutes, stirring often, then reduce the heat to medium; simmer just until the rhubarb is beginning to fall apart, about 3 minutes. Remove from the heat.

Stir in the remaining strawberries. Cool. Chill until cold, at least 1 hour and up to 1 day. Serve over pancakes or waffles, inside a sweet crêpe or with scones.

GUINNESS CHOCOLATE SAUCE

This unusual version of chocolate sauce uses Guinness stout with its caramel and honey notes and underlying toastiness. This sauce is as delicious mixed with milk for chocolate milk as it is over ice cream.

MAKES: 1 cup (240 ml) **PREP TIME:** 5 minutes **COOK TIME:** 10 minutes

¾ cup (150 g) granulated sugar

Pinch of salt

½ cup (43 g) unsweetened cocoa powder

1 cup (240 ml) Guinness stout

1½ cups (270 g) semisweet chocolate chips

2 tsp (10 ml) vanilla

In a small saucepan, whisk together the sugar, salt, cocoa powder and Guinness. Bring to a boil and turn down and allow to simmer for about 5 minutes.

Remove the pot from the heat and whisk in the chocolate chips and the vanilla. Cool completely and serve over vanilla ice cream or a brownie sundae. Store unused sauce in an airtight container in the refrigerator.

SALTED COCONUT SUGAR CARAMEL SAUCE

This vegan caramel sauce is sure to please everyone with its hint of coconut taste and salty notes. We like to use Hawaiian pink sea salt in this sauce, but the more readily available Himalayan pink sea salt works well too. Serve this sauce over angel food cake, pound cake or vanilla ice cream, or use as a drizzle on top of a caramel sundae or whipped cream on a coffee drink or hot cocoa.

Coconut sugar is crystallized from boiled coconut nectar in a process similar to extracting sugar crystals from sugar cane juice. Unlike regular sugar, however, coconut sugar has a low glycemic index, which makes it a better choice for those watching their sugar intake. Coconut sugar is available at gourmet and health food markets.

MAKES: 1 cup (240 ml)　　**PREP TIME:** 5 minutes　　**COOK TIME:** 30 minutes

¾ cup (108 g) coconut sugar

¾ cup (180 ml) water

½ cup (120 ml) coconut cream

½ tsp vanilla

¼ tsp Hawaiian pink sea salt or Himalayan pink salt

Bring the coconut sugar and water to a boil in a small saucepan and then reduce to a simmer. Simmer until the mixture reduces by half, about 4 to 5 minutes.

Add the coconut cream and whisk very well. Scrape the sides of the saucepan down with a rubber spatula. Reduce the heat to low and continue to simmer, stirring occasionally, for 20 to 22 minutes or until the mixture forms a thick caramel sauce. Remove from heat and stir in the vanilla and salt. Drizzle warm sauce over ice cream, cake, pie, brownies or coffee drinks.

CANDIED GINGER AND APRICOT SAUCE

This elegant sauce came about after experimenting with dried apricots and candied ginger in a bread pudding that was spiced with cardamom and served with a saffron rosewater crème anglaise. The combination of tart, aromatic and astringent flavors was so heavenly it seemed a shame not harness them in a more a versatile form for use with a variety of other desserts.

The end result is this syrup, which features apricot brandy as well as apricot preserves. Serve this as a glaze for donuts and fried dough or cakes, as a topping for vanilla ice cream, or brush on custard tarts or cheesecake prior to garnishing with fresh fruit. It's also excellent on waffles, crêpes and pancakes. Of course, it's great with bread pudding too!

MAKES: ¾ cup (180 ml)　　**PREP TIME:** 10 minutes　　**COOK TIME:** 30 minutes

½ cup (120 ml) water

1 tbsp (6 g) grated candied ginger

¼ tsp ground saffron

¼ cup apricot preserves

1 cup (200 g) sugar

¼ tsp cardamom

½ tsp rosewater

1 tbsp (15 ml) apricot brandy

Combine the water, candied ginger and saffron in a small saucepan over medium heat. Simmer for 5 to 6 minutes or until the mixture reduces to 1 cup (240 ml).

Add the preserves and sugar and stir while the mixture is simmering until the sugar is dissolved and the preserves are melted. Simmer for 18 to 20 minutes until the mixture thickens to a syrup. Stir in the cardamom, rosewater and apricot brandy and whisk well. Cool and store in an airtight container. Serve with waffles, pancakes, cheesecake, bread pudding or fresh fruit.

RUMMY FRUIT COMPOUND BUTTER

This fruit butter is based on the initial steps toward making Black Cake, a Caribbean Christmas cake for which Ramin is famous among our friends and family. The cake calls for dried fruits soaked in rum and puréed then added to a cake batter made with plenty of butter. Normally, the fruits for the cake are soaked for weeks and weeks but we've developed a quick method using a microwave to approximate the same flavors. Although it may seem counterintuitive, use a salted butter for this compound butter because the touch of salt enhances the sweet and rummy flavors.

This butter is excellent on everything from muffins to waffles and pancakes. It's even good on toast. Gently toasted nuts mixed with a little bit of this butter, melted, are a delicious topping for Danish and pound cake too.

MAKES: 4 ounces (112 g)   **PREP TIME:** 10 minutes   **COOK TIME:** 5 minutes

1 tbsp (10 g) dark raisins, minced

1 tbsp (10 g) dried cherries, minced

4 pitted prunes, minced

½ cup (120 ml) spiced rum

8 tbsp (120 g) salted butter, softened

1 tbsp (14 g) dark brown sugar

1 tsp (3 g) ground cinnamon

⅛ tsp ground allspice

⅛ tsp ground cloves

Mix the fruits together in a small microwave-safe bowl and add the rum. Cover tightly with plastic wrap and microwave on high for 1 to 1½ minutes, or until the plastic wrap begins to suction to the bowl. Remove the bowl from the microwave and set aside until it is completely cool.

Place the butter in the bowl of a stand mixer and add the sugar, cinnamon, allspice and cloves. Mix for 1 minute or until all the ingredients are well combined. Alternatively, you may do this with a whisk by hand.

Drain the rum from the fruits and add the fruit to the butter mixture. Discard the rum or keep to drizzle on vanilla ice cream. Mix the fruits well into the butter.

Scrape the butter into a small bowl and cover tightly with plastic wrap. Alternatively, cut a square of wax paper 12 inches by 12 inches (30 by 30 cm) and scoop the butter into the center of the paper. Fold the wax paper over the butter and roll forward to form a log. Twist the ends of the wax paper tightly. Chill the butter until solid. The butter may also be frozen for later use. It will keep up to 1 month in the freezer. Use slices of butter on warm muffins, scones, waffles or pancakes.

FIVE-SPICE AND BROWN SUGAR COMPOUND BUTTER

In this recipe, brown sugar combines with the warmly aromatic flavors of Chinese five-spice powder, which features anise, cinnamon, Sichuan pepper, fennel and cloves and is available in Asian markets. This particular mix is well balanced enough for both sweet and savory uses, but you can increase or decrease the amount of sugar to achieve a more sweet or savory profile to your taste.

MAKES: 4 ounces (112 g)   **PREP TIME:** 1 minute   **COOK TIME:** 3 to 4 minutes

8 tbsp (120 g) unsalted butter, softened

1 tbsp (5 g) dark brown sugar

Pinch of salt

1½ tsp (5 g) five-spice powder

Place the butter, sugar and salt in the bowl of a stand mixer and whip on medium for 2 to 3 minutes or until the mixture is fluffy. You may also place the ingredients in a medium bowl and whip with a hand mixer.

Add the five-spice powder and whip for 30 seconds more.

Scrape the mixture into a ramekin or small bowl and press down gently to remove any bubbles. Smooth the top and wrap tightly in plastic wrap.

Chill until firm, about 2 to 3 hours. This will keep for 2 to 3 weeks, refrigerated. Use on waffles, pancakes, warm muffins or French toast.

Dipping SAUCES

Dipping sauces—whether for the main course or as part of an appetizer or party plate—add fun to eating. From the smallest kid to the oldest adult, there's something a bit decadent about dipping a morsel into a sauce that will provide an extra burst of flavor or texture.

Here we offer various dips that are a unique take on classics like tomato salsa, hummus or cheese spread—ideal for chips, crackers or crudités.

CHINESE SCALLION AND GINGER SAUCE

This sauce is a great example of how the simplest preparations can offer the most complex tastes. This sauce is usually served as an accompaniment to dim sum in Chinese restaurants, and it is surely addictive. It's great with dumplings, spring rolls and savory crêpes as well as pan-seared meats or stir-fried vegetables. It's so good you'll find yourself looking for things to put it on. Best of all, it's incredibly easy to prepare.

MAKES: ½ cup (120 ml)   **PREP TIME:** 10 minutes   **COOKING TIME:** 3 minutes

½ cup (120 ml) safflower oil

1 (2-inch [5-cm]) piece of ginger, grated

5 scallions, trimmed and minced finely

Heat the safflower oil in a small saucepan over low heat and add the ginger and scallions. Gently heat this mixture for 3 to 4 minutes but do not allow the vegetables to fry.

Remove from the heat when the sauce becomes aromatic. Cool and serve slightly warm or room temperature as a condiment or dipping sauce with finger foods like dumplings, shumai, spring or summer rolls.

TAMARIND AND DATE SAUCE

Lovers of Indian food will recognize this tamarind and date sauce as a popular condiment for fried snacks such as samosas—the vegetable- or meat-stuffed triangular turnover. However, this sauce is also excellent as a dip for fried chicken wings or shrimp kebabs. It can also be spooned over seared chicken breast or filet mignon. Dates provide a sweet counterpoint to extremely sour tamarind paste, but you'll still need a little tempering in the form of brown sugar. As always, feel free to add more cayenne pepper than is called for in the recipe, if you choose.

MAKES: 1 cup (240 ml)　　**PREP TIME:** 10 minutes　　**COOK TIME:** 30 to 35 minutes

12 pitted dates, preferably medjool

1½ cups (360 ml) water

½ cup (120 ml) tamarind paste

3 tbsp (41 g) dark brown sugar

1 tsp (3 g) cayenne powder

1 tsp (3 g) ginger powder

1 tsp (3 g) ground cumin

½ tsp salt or more to taste

Roughly chop the dates and combine them with 1½ cups (360 ml) of water in a medium saucepan. Bring to a simmer and simmer until the dates are soft and beginning to break apart, about 15 to 20 minutes.

Stir in the tamarind paste, dark brown sugar, cayenne, ginger and cumin and simmer for 7 to 10 minutes or until the mixture is reduced by one quarter.

Add the salt and stir well. Pour mixture into a blender or food processor and puree to a smooth paste. Pour purée through a fine mesh sieve to remove any pieces of date skins and then add the purée back into the same saucepan. Simmer for 5 minutes more, cool completely before serving with samosas, chicken wings or other fried snacks.

BASBAAS

BasBaas is a spicy Somali sauce served mainly as a condiment to enhance otherwise mild Somali cuisine. In many ways, it is reminiscent of Indian cilantro chutney with a bright zing from lime juice. This is another one of those preparations that can be used as a dip, a condiment or as a traditional sauce on grilled seafood or chicken. We like to use Thai green chilies in our version, but you can use a mix of green chilies that suit your taste. Green habañero peppers make for a spicier sauce while jalapeño peppers are the basis for a somewhat milder sauce.

MAKES: about ¾ cup (180 ml)   **PREP TIME:** 5 minutes   **COOK TIME:** None

5 Thai green chilies

1 shallot

3 cloves garlic

Juice of 1 lime

1 bunch cilantro, leaves only

¼ tsp freshly ground black pepper

½ tsp salt

¼ cup (60 ml) white vinegar or more as needed

Combine the chilies, shallot, garlic, lime, cilantro, black pepper and salt in a food processor and process to a rough paste.

Add the vinegar and process to a smooth thick purée, adding more as needed to achieve this consistency. Store in a sealed, nonreactive container in the refrigerator. Serve as a condiment with fried snacks. It's extremely good with French fries or yuca fries.

TROPICAL FRUIT SALSA

Salsa is one of America's most popular chip dips, but it could easily be so much more. We've created this version that pairs the usual tomato, chilies and onions with tropical fruit for a touch of sweetness and tang. This combination featuring mango, pineapple and papaya is great not just as a dip but also as a topping for grilled chicken, seafood and even pork.

MAKES: about 3 cups (720 ml)

PREP TIME: 15 minutes

COOK TIME: None

3 roma tomatoes, chopped roughly

½ cup (120 ml) mango chunks

½ cup (120 ml) pineapple chunks

½ cup (120 ml) papaya chunks

½ bunch cilantro, leaves only

1 small onion, minced

3 cloves garlic, minced

Juice of 2 limes

½ tsp cayenne powder

½ tsp salt

Place the tomatoes, mango, pineapple, papaya and cilantro in a food processor and pulse to a rough purée.

Scrape the mixture into a medium bowl and add the onions, garlic, lime juice, cayenne and salt. Mix well and cover. Refrigerate at least 2 hours before using. Store in an airtight container in the refrigerator. Use over grilled meats or as a dip with tortilla chips.

COCONUT WITH HARISSA DIPPING SAUCE

This is an excellent sauce for any small fried bites such as tempura vegetables or fried shrimp. It's also excellent with spring rolls and even dumplings. Harissa is a spicy red pepper paste that is common to North African cuisine. You can find it in Middle Eastern grocery stores or gourmet markets. Coconut nectar, which is sometimes called coconut molasses, is available in gourmet and health food markets. It imparts a lightly sweet, and slightly smoky flavor without being overpowering.

MAKES: 1 cup (240 ml)   **PREP TIME:** 5 minutes   **COOK TIME:** 3 to 5 minutes

1 tsp (5 ml) toasted sesame oil

½ shallot, minced

1 tbsp (9 g) grated fresh ginger

¼ cup (60 ml) rice wine or sake

½ tsp harissa, or more as desired

¾ cup (180 ml) coconut nectar

Heat the sesame oil in a medium saucepan over medium-low heat. Add the shallot and ginger and sauté for 1 minute. Stir in the rice wine and cook until the mixture is reduced by half, 1 to 2 minutes.

Mix in the harissa and coconut nectar. Simmer for 2 minutes longer, stirring well. Remove from the heat and allow to cool slightly. Serve with fried foods like dumplings, spring rolls or chicken wings.

BUYING GUIDE

ALEGRO FOODS: (www.alegrofoods.com) A comprehensive online resource for Mexican and Spanish Caribbean ingredients.

H MART: (www.hmart.com) Originally a New Jersey–based Korean supermarket, H Mart has national locations and online sales and offers a wide range of East and Southeast Asian products.

KALUSTYAN'S: (www.kalustyans.com) This 70-plus-year-old New York City gourmet market features a wide variety of international ingredients with an emphasis on South Asian and Middle Eastern goods.

KING ARTHUR FLOUR: (www.kingarthurflour.com) King Arthur Flour sells a variety of specialty flours as well as extracts, seasonings and flavorings for both sweet and savory preparations.

PENZEYS SPICES: (www.penzeys.com) The international spice seller with both brick and mortar shops and online sales, offers quantities as little as one ounce (28 g)—good for experimenting.

THE PERFECT PURÉE OF NAPA VALLEY: (www.perfectpuree.com) A chef's favorite, Perfect Purée offers frozen and refrigerated puréed fruits, concentrates and zests in both standard flavors like peach, strawberry, apricot, cranberry and apple as well more exotic flavors like coconut, passion fruit, guava, lychee and prickly pear.

PATEL BROTHERS: (www.patelbros.com) A South Asian supermarket with stores and online shopping, Patel Brothers is a good source for Indian and some Middle Eastern ingredients. Bulk spices in various sizes provide good value.

GLOSSARY

CASSAREEP: A thick, dark sauce made from yuca (cassava), a tropical tuber and additional spices. It is most often used as the base of stews in Caribbean and Guyanese cooking.

COCONUT CREAM: Coconut cream is the thickest form of coconut milk, a preparation made from puréeing fresh coconuts and water together into a thick paste. It may be thinned with water to achieve various consistencies of coconut milk. Coconut cream is readily available in most supermarkets.

COCONUT MILK: Coconut milk is made from puréeing fresh coconut milk and water together and then straining the resulting thick white liquid in a fine sieve, mesh bag or cheesecloth to create milk. Like coconut cream, it's widely available in most supermarkets.

COCONUT NECTAR: Also called coconut molasses, this syrup is the boiled sap of the coconut tree. Similar in consistency to maple syrup, coconut nectar has a somewhat smoky taste.

DEGLAZE: The process of removing the browned bits of meat (fond) at the bottom of a sauté pan or roasting pan using an acidic liquid such as wine, vinegar or citrus juice.

DUKKAH: An Egyptian spice mixture of toasted nuts along with fennel, coriander, dried pepper and herbs. Dukkah is used as both a seasoning for meats and fish as well as a dip, along with olive oil, for bread and raw vegetables.

DUTCH PROCESS/ULTRA-DUTCHED COCOA: Dutching is the process of removing alkaline from cocoa powder. The result is a darker, less bitter cocoa powder.

EMULSIFICATION: A preparation in which oil and liquid are forced together in a cohesive form.

EUROPEAN STYLE BUTTER: A general term to refer to butter that has a higher level of fat and less water. The higher fat levels contribute to smoother, more velvety sauce.

FENUGREEK: An herb used in Middle Eastern and South Asian cooking that has an aroma similar to maple syrup and a savory taste.

FIVE-SPICE POWDER: A Chinese seasoning powder of Sichuan peppercorns, fennel seeds, cinnamon, star anise and clove used in everything from meats to vegetables to desserts.

FOND: The browned or caramelized pieces of meat and drippings created on the bottom of a sauté pan used to sear meat or a roasting pan used to cook meat.

GARAM MASALA: A classic Indian spice mixture in which various spices including pepper, cloves, cinnamon, mace, bay leaf, cumin and brown and green cardamom pods are toasted then ground together. The name means warm (garam) mix (masala). Garam masalas can vary from region to region and comprise a different percentage of spices or different spices in the mix, including cloves, fennel seeds, coriander seeds, chilies and other regional favorites.

GHEE: Also called clarified butter, ghee is butter that has been melted and cooked slowly over a low temperature to cook off the milk solids. The resulting butter acts more like a vegetable oil with a higher scorch point and a clear appearance.

GOCHUJANG: A spicy paste made from the Korean gochugaru chili pepper. A common flavoring in Korean cuisine.

HABAÑERO PEPPER: Also called Scotch Bonnet pepper. An extremely spicy chili pepper used often in Caribbean and African cuisine.

NAPPÉ: The ideal consistency of a sauce in which it is thick enough to lightly coat the back of a spoon without dripping and will, as a result, evenly coat food.

MEYER LEMON: A sweeter milder lemon with a thinner, egg yolk colored skin. Highly aromatic, Meyer lemons originated in China and are now widely cultivated in California.

MISO PASTE: Miso is fermented soy bean curd and is available in white, brown or red varieties. Highly salty, miso can be the basis of soup or add an umami aspect to sauces and stews.

MONTER AU BEURRE (MOUNT WITH BUTTER): A French term referring to the practice of finishing a sauce with a small amount of butter for sheen and velvety texture.

PIMENTE D'ESPELETTE: A small, mild chili pepper originating in Central and South America and brought to France during the colonial era. Over time, the pepper has become integral to the cuisine of Basque shepherds in Northern Spain. It is available dried whole, powdered or pickled.

POMEGRANATE MOLASSES OR SYRUP: A thick, sweet-sour syrup made from pomegranate juice that is often used in Middle Eastern cooking.

SEVILLE ORANGES: A bitter orange used for juice to add to stews and sauces or to marinate fish and meats. It is often marketed as Bitter Orange Juice in 750 milliliter glass bottles.

SOURSOP: A tropical fruit with a hard green shell, large seeds and a creamy off-white interior. Naturally sweet and sour, soursop is most often used in shakes and desserts.

TANDOORI SEASONING: Also called Tandoori Masala, this is an Indian spice mix that features chili pepper and paprika (for red coloring) as well as turmeric, cumin, ginger, coriander and sometimes, nutmeg and cinnamon. Tandoori seasoning is the flavoring agent for many Indian barbecue meat dishes.

UMAMI: One of the five taste sensations (the others being hot, sour, salty and sweet). Umami is a Japanese expression that describes the taste of meatiness such as from a grilled steak, fish sauce or soy sauce.

ACKNOWLEDGMENTS

Thanks to Page Street for being as excited about sauces as we are—that is why you are holding this book in your hands.

Whenever writing a cookbook, the process of creating and testing recipes means you have to enlist a lot of tasters for the task, so thank you to all our family and friends who put their taste buds to work on behalf of this book.

Thanks too, to the many great fellow chefs and creative home cooks we've both had the pleasure of working with over the years—you are always an inspiration.

The most special thanks goes to Food Network celebrity host Ted Allen who introduced us via Facebook many years ago. Little did he know he was the agent of a bond based in cooking that has blossomed into a sisterhood.

ABOUT THE AUTHORS

Lorilynn Bauer is a private chef and TV personality who has worked in the finest restaurants and homes across America including Bayona, in New Orleans; Postino, in California; and the Lodge at Koele and Manele Bay in Lanai, Hawaii, among others. She spent four years on *Iron Chef America* as the sous chef for her friend and colleague Cat Cora—the first female Iron Chef. In addition to her television appearances she is a world traveler, immersing herself in the food styles of multiple cultures to bring a depth of flavor and unique experience to her cooking. Lorilynn attended the Culinary Institute of America.

Ramin Ganeshram is an award-winning journalist and cookbook author who specializes in food culture. She has written for *Saveur, Epicurious, National Geographic Traveler* and many others. Ramin has written about everything from soul food to all the uses for coconut and more. This is her seventh cookbook. Ramin attended the Institute of Culinary Education and holds a master's degree from Columbia University Graduate School of Journalism.

INDEX